ChilDReN's COTTAGE

CookieBook

Everything you need to know about cookies.

written and edited by
Norma Bannerman, PHEc and Shirley Rebus, PHEc

CHiLdren'S COTTAGE CookieBook

Written and edited by
Norma Bannerman, PHEc
Shirley Rebus, PHEc

Canadian Cataloguing in Publication Data
Rebus, Shirley, 1946 –
  Children's Cottage cookie cookbook

ISBN 0-9696478-0-8

1. Cookies. I. Bannerman, Norma.
II. Children's Cottage Society of Calgary.
III. Title.
TX772.R42 1992   641.8'654   C92-091734-8

First Printing - October 1992

Published by
Children's Cottage
  Society of Calgary
Calgary, Alberta

Printed by
Mountain View Printing
& Graphics Ltd.
4724 – 14 Street NE
Calgary, Alberta   T2E 6L7
(403) 291-9353

Desktop publishing by
Cowboy and Me Publishing Co.
1403 – 105 Avenue SW
Calgary, Alberta   T2W 0B5
(403) 252-7191

Photography by
Hutchinson & Company
Upstairs, 1210 – 11 Avenue SW
Calgary, Alberta   T3C 0M4
(403) 229-0487

The Nickle Family Foundation is gratefully acknowledged, for funding the printing of this cookbook, and for their strong commitment to the care and nurture of children and to the prevention of child abuse and neglect. Their generosity provides an opportunity for many to support the work of the Children's Cottage.

Text and divider pages printed on recycled paper.

Designed, printed and produced in Canada.

Pat Dougan, MSW, RSW
Director, Child Abuse Program
Alberta Children's Hospital
Honorary Patron, Children's Cottage

On Behalf of the Children's Cottage

The Children's Cottage is a crisis nursery that offers a safe and friendly homelike environment for babies and pre-school children during times of family crisis and stress. Since it opened in December 1986, the cottage has sheltered 4000 children. Unfortunately, it has turned away the same number due to lack of space. The Child Abuse Program at Alberta Children's Hospital believes the Children's Cottage provides a crucial service to children at risk and to their families. We frequently advise our clientele about the cottage and its services, as many parents experiencing high stress often require concrete assistance and parenting relief to ensure the safety and well-being of their young children.

The Children's Cottage is not a babysitting service. Rather, it is a place where parents can bring their children to ensure their safety while parents regain a level of patience and tolerance or work out their problems. They may be facing such crises as a sudden illness or hospitalization, marital conflict, housing problems, fear of hurting or neglecting their child, serious financial difficulties, or feelings of isolation and depression which could interfere with safe parenting.

Your interest, concern and participation is very much needed. By supporting the Children's Cottage you will help families help themselves. You will also reduce the risk faced by many fragile and vulnerable children. It is particularly on behalf of those children that I sincerely thank you for your help and support.

A Big Thank You!

The writing, production and marketing of this book has been a gigantic volunteer effort. To all who have participated, your energy and enthusiasm were appreciated. It was a project made possible by your generous gift of time and expertise. We thank

...the people who got the ball rolling

Jeanette Sutherland, for the wonderful idea of a cookie cookbook.

Marilyn Clark, Vice President, Member and Public Relations, Calgary Co-op, for her support of the concept.

Linda Whitworth, for her enthusiasm in bringing others to this project.

...the editors, who created this book, coordinated the recipe testing, and proof-read an enormous number of pages.

Norma Bannerman and Shirley Rebus

...the desktop publisher, who designed the layout and did all the typesetting with immense patience.

Nollind van Bryce, of Cowboy and Me Publishing Co.

...the photographer, who brought our recipes to life.

Ross Hutchinson, of Hutchinson and Company

...the food stylist, who cheerfully prepared food and designed layouts for the photo sessions.

Linda Whitworth, home economist, Calgary Co-op.

...the artist, whose drawings add vitality to the book.

Brandie Cormier

...the professional home economists, members of the Alberta Home Economics Association, Calgary Branch, who tested the recipes.

Laurie Alisat	Lynne Glata	Joan MacFarlane
Faye Forbes Anderson	Joanne Good	Shirley Rebus
Norma Bannerman	Sheila Heinrich	Diane Rennie
Carolyn Berkan	Joan Hickie	Kathy Simpson
Dora Blitt	(assisted by Julie)	Arlene Smith
Debbie Brekke	Linda Homenick	Susan Somerville
Jane Carlyle	Marcia Inch	Sharon Speranza
Marilyn Clark	Pat Inglis	Susan Spicer
Kathy Deyell	Sylvia Kong	Louise Starling
Fran Genereux	Audrey Kuzyk	Cindy von Hagen
(assisted by Nicole)	Marjorie Laurence	Linda Whitworth

...those who provided written information

Fran Genereux, for cookie-making with kids.

Patti Rathwell, for microwave oven information.

...the reviewers ot the draft manuscript, for their perspectives.

Judy Dyke, Children's Cottage
Sandra Mapp, Children's Cottage
Cynny Willet, food writer, Calgary Herald
Joanne Good, freelance food writer
Nadine Ryan-Bannerman, adult education consultant

...the accountant, who is keeping track of it all.

Bob Bannerman

...the members of the marketing and promotion committees, who are ensuring that word gets out about this book.

Judy Dyke	Jeanette Sutherland	Debbie Brekke
Joanne Good	Jennifer Reilly	Colleen Klein
Sandra Mapp		Leianne Vye-Rogers

...the volunteer coordinator, who is recruiting and organizing people.

Morgan Tarves

...the wonderful volunteers, who are working at malls, craft fairs, and business locations to make this book widely and readily available.

...the distribution coordinators, who are keeping inventory and making sure books are where they are supposed to be.

Bob Bannerman	Kevin Gibbons
Michael Denis	Clifford Wilson

...those who submitted recipes

Faye Forbes Anderson	Freda Fledderjohn	Dorotka Kjersteen	Nadine Ryan-
Wendy Aylesworth	Fran Genereux	Jeanne Kolody	Bannerman
Norma Bannerman	Colleen Ghercim	Patricia Kolody	Flo Sinner
Bunny Barss	Lynne Glata	Audrey Kuzyk	Arlene Smith
Dora Blitt	Joanne Good	Norma Lake	Gay Smithson
Cathy Cochrane	Grandma!	Sandra Mapp	Betty Summers
Colleen Cousens	Kerri Hale	Mom!	Barb Van Fossen
Joan Craven	Nancy Hay	Shelley Mennis	Leone Van Fossen
Anne Dand	Linda Homenick	Debbi Nichizaki	Verna
Kathy Deyell	Bev Hubick	Shirley Rebus	Edith Whitworth
Elsie Dyke	Pat Inglis	Jennifer Reilly	Cynny Willet
Judy Dyke	Glenda Jones	Sandra Reilly	Betty Wolfe
Louise Dyke	Marion Kelly	Audrey Rezanoff	Gertie Zorn
Laura Edwards	Gail Kent	Mary Richmond	
Donna Flanagan	Patty Kilgallon	Marlene Rink	

...and the friends, family, neighbours and co-workers who made up our taste panels.

Norma Bannerman, Shirley Rebus

Thoughts about cookies

In the process of writing this book, we talked to a lot of people about cookies. Along the way, we discovered that cookie-related experiences have a special place in peoples' memories. One woman recalled the warm feeling of being allowed to climb on her grandmother's knee to dunk cookies in tea. A 70-year-old man insisted that Chinese Chews *had* to be shaped into rolls rather than balls—because that's how his mother always made them.

We trust that the recipes in this book will help you recapture fond memories and perhaps start new traditions—mailing cookies to a young person living away from home, exchanging cookies with friends to turn holiday baking into a cooperative experience, or making cookies with children, either your's or someone else's, for both the pleasure of it and to give them an opportunity to experience the satisfaction of creating something themselves. This is more than a recipe book. It is a book about cooking in its broadest sense—caring, loving and giving.

...and this project

It has been a privilege to participate in all phases of the production of this book—the meetings, planning, testing, tasting, writing, proof-reading, networking—and finally the birth of this"baby" we had envisioned. As editors we enjoyed working together, and were constantly energized and encouraged by the enthusiasm of other members of the steering committee, particularly chairman Judy Dyke.

Early on we developed some clear criteria. Only recipes that tasted "more-ish" would be included—meaning that each cookie or bar under scrutiny had to taste so good we simply couldn't stop at one. In addition, we wanted users of this book to have confidence in the recipes, the instructions, and ultimately in themselves and their own abilities and creativity. To this end, all recipes were tested carefully by a small army of home economists, we endeavoured to write the recipes as clearly as possible, and we included information that hopefully will clear up dilemmas which readers might have experienced in the past. In other words, we wanted this book to be "user-friendly."

Creating the *Children's Cottage Cookie Cook Book* has been a labour of love; many individuals gave the best of their time and abilities to produce it. We are confident you are receiving good value in this book—and perhaps an even greater value will be in knowing that you have helped young children in crisis situations.

From all of us, but especially from the children who need the Cottage— **THANKS!**

Contents

For Good Results

Things You Need to Know

Sometimes two people using the same recipe create finished products that are quite different. Even experienced cooks occasionally find that things seem to change right in their own kitchens!

Big differences in the finished product can result from apparently small differences in ovens, cookie sheets and baking pans, measuring utensils and techniques, or ingredients.

Oven temperature may not always be what the dial says. Because a few degrees too hot or too cool will affect baking time and appearance, it may be necessary to set temperature dial higher or lower.

Cookie sheets and baking pans vary in weight, colour and baking qualities.

Dark-coloured pans bake cookies more quickly and may give a dark-coloured product, particularly on the bottom.

Light-coloured pans are slower bakers; cookies are generally more lightly and evenly browned.

Lightweight pans bake cookies more quickly than heavier ones and are more likely to cause overbrowning.

Double or triple layered cookie sheets, a recent innovation, are designed to slow down baking and promote even browning. Cookies may take a minute or two longer to bake on these sheets.

Small variations in flour and liquid can affect the consistency of cookie doughs. This explains why cookies made from the same recipe sometimes spread too much and at other times are too dry and don't spread enough. A number of factors cause these variations:

Flour is affected by the humidity of the environment. In Calgary, where humidity is generally very *low*, flour dries out quickly. When flour is dry it absorbs extra moisture from the dough; therefore, less flour may be required than called for in the recipe. In regions where humidity is *high*, flour absorbs moisture from the environment. When this moist flour is used in baking, it in turn adds extra moisture to the dough. To compensate for this extra moisture, it might be necessary to add more flour than called for in the recipe. Once a bag of flour is opened, atmospheric conditions determine whether flour dries out or takes on moisture. Storing flour in an airtight container maintains a more constant moisture content.

Flour can vary in gluten content from crop to crop, depending on the gluten present in the grain from which it is made. Since gluten combines with water in doughs, the gluten content of the flour affects moisture-absorbing qualities.

Eggs contribute moisture to dough. Switching between medium and large eggs can affect dough consistency. Either can be used, but the flour level may have to be adjusted since most recipes do not indicate the size of eggs used originally.

Honey and molasses can vary in moisture content.

Measuring techniques and utensils are important, as inaccuracies will affect dough consistency.

Measuring techniques are described on page 8.

Nested measuring cups present a dilemma. Most are calibrated in imperial and metric, for example 1 cup and 250 mL, on the same utensil. Since 1 cup actually equals 237 mL, a utensil marked with both 1 cup and 250 mL will be correct in either imperial *or* metric, but not both. We recommend using nested cups which are calibrated in one system only. If these are not available, be aware of the inaccuracies of measures calibrated in both systems, and adjust the flour as needed.

None of these is a major problem. You simply need to do the following:

• **Become familiar with your own oven, baking equipment and utensils, and make the necessary adjustments.**

• **When preparing cookie dough, add the last of the flour gradually until desired dough consistency is reached. If uncertain, it is better for dough to be slightly soft rather than too stiff. It is easier to add a little extra flour than to work in extra liquid.**

• **Always bake a test cookie before baking a full pan of cookies.**

What Ingredients Do

Flour provides structure and body for baked products. In most cases, all-purpose and whole wheat flour can be successfully substituted one for the other. In plain cookies there is a slight flavour change when whole wheat flour is used, but people who use whole wheat flour regularly appreciate this difference. When using whole wheat flour in baked products for the first time, you may prefer to begin by using half all-purpose and half whole wheat flour.

Sweeteners affect texture and flavour.

White sugar makes cookies crisper.

Brown sugar makes cookies a little softer because it contains molasses.

Honey and molasses make cookies considerably softer because they are liquid at room temperature.

Fats contribute to the tenderness or shortness of baked products and help to carry the flavours provided by spices and flavourings. Most cookies and bars contain some kind of fat. Oil is occasionally used, but most often the fat is butter, margarine or shortening.

Butter, since it is made from milk, contains some milk solids and water.

Solid margarine is made from vegetable oil and has milk solids added to give it a flavour more comparable to butter. Like butter, margarine contains some water.

Soft margarines, that is margarines that are still soft when refrigerated, are also made from vegetable oil. However, some of the oil is left in the liquid state, making the margarine soft and spreadable when chilled. Some fat-reduced margarines contain extra water or milk. These extra liquids can alter the flour-liquid ratio in a recipe, resulting in a different product.

Use solid margarine in baking unless the recipe has either been developed for use with a soft margarine or has been successfully adjusted to compensate for the extra liquid.

Shortenings, like margarines, are made from vegetable oil—unlike margarines they contain neither milk solids nor water. Shortenings have somewhat more tenderizing power than butter and margarine but contribute very little flavour.

Most of the recipes in this book call for butter or margarine. Both give good results. When a recipe contains other ingredients such as cocoa, molasses or spices, you may not recognize whether butter or margarine has been used. If it is a product such as shortbread where there are no other ingredients competing for flavour, we suggest using butter for *its* flavour. This is why you will find a few recipes in this book where only butter is listed. However, the choice is yours. If you prefer margarine, by all means use it.

Whichever fat you use—butter, margarine or shortening—the quantity to be used in the recipe is the same.

Making a Recipe Your Own

Some ingredients such as flour, oats, sugar, fat, egg and leavenings should remain as the recipe is written. But there is tremendous scope for change within the other ingredients used in cookies and bars.

Spices and flavourings are added to create flavours pleasing to your palate. However, if a recipe calls for a spice or flavouring that you don't like, but you think you'd like the recipe otherwise, then leave it out or substitute one you do like. Obviously it will be different from the original recipe, but you will have created something *you* like better.

Dried fruits, nuts, seeds and chocolate chips can be exchanged, substituted, mixed and matched to suit individual tastes. There is really no law about this! If you don't like dates or candied cherries, but love raisins, then use raisins instead. Nuts are generally interchangeable, and sunflower seeds are often a good substitute. Chocolate chips add their own unique flavour. When you change an ingredient to suit your taste buds, you have created a recipe that is your own.

Baking a Test Cookie

Shape or drop one cookie as directed in the recipe. Baking this cookie allows you to check shape and colour to determine if any adjustments are needed in consistency of dough, baking time, or temperature setting of your oven.

Check	Observation	Solution
Shape	Spreads too much	Mix in 1 - 2 tablespoons (15 - 25 mL) flour.
	Does not spread when it should	Blend in 2 - 3 teaspoons (10 - 15 mL) water or milk.
Colour	Too dark on bottom	Move rack nearer top of oven, turn down temperature by 25°F (10°C), and/or use lighter-coloured or multiple layered cookie sheet.
	Overbrowned in specified baking time	Reduce oven temperature by 25°F (10°C) and/or shorten baking time.
	Underbaked in specified baking time	Increase oven temperature by 25°F (10°C) and/or increase baking time.

Children's Cottage Cookie Cook Book

Bar Cookies

Doubling or Halving Bar Recipes

- Double or halve the *ingredient quantities.*

- Use the *correct size pan,* as indicated in the chart below. When doubling a recipe and baking it in a 10 x 15-inch (25 x 40 cm) jelly roll pan, be sure the pan is deep enough.

- *Baking temperature* remains the same.

- *Baking time* may need to be increased or decreased by a few minutes, but remains surprisingly constant. For example, our Fudge Brownies are baked in an 8-inch (20 cm) square pan at 375°F (190°C) for 30 minutes. The doubled recipe, in a 9 x 13-inch (22 x 34 cm) pan, bakes perfectly at the same temperature for the same length of time.

- The same criteria for *judging doneness* apply except when doubling or halving recipes using 10 x 15-inch (25 x 40 cm) jelly roll pans. Most of these pans have shallow sides, resulting in faster browning. Consequently, colour may not be a reliable guide for judging doneness. If unsure, insert a cake tester in the centre or test by touching lightly with your finger.

Original recipe	Doubled recipe	Original recipe	Halved recipe
8-inch square (20 cm) square	9 x 13 inch (22 x 34 cm)	9 x 13 inch (22 x 34 cm)	8-inch square (20 cm) square
9-inch square (22 cm) square	10 x 15 inch (25 x 40 cm)	10 x 15 inch (25 x 40 cm)	9-inch square (22 cm) square

Cutting Bars

Bar cookies are typically cut into bars and squares, but can also be made into thin strips or triangles. Triangles are created by cutting squares, then cutting each in half diagonally.

The yield from a pan of bars depends on how large or small the pieces are. On average, a square pan will make about 2 dozen and a 9 x 13-inch (22 x 34 cm) pan will make 3 to 4 dozen.

Measuring Ingredients

Utensils

Nested measuring cup sets are designed to accurately measure dry ingredients such as flour and sugar. Simply fill the cup heaping full and level off the surface with a knife or spatula.

Glass measuring cups are used for all liquids. To obtain an accurate measure, set on a level surface and read at eye level.

It is difficult to accurately measure dry ingredients in a glass cup or liquid ingredients in nested cups. Since a small variation in liquid or flour can make a significant difference in cookie doughs, it is a worthwhile investment to have both types in your kitchen.

Ingredients

Flour is pre-sifted during manufacture, so sifting is not necessary in most recipes. It should, however, be handled lightly. If flour has become compacted, stir before measuring.

Brown sugar should be scooped into measuring cup and lightly pressed.

Hard butter can't be pressed into a measuring cup, but there are two easy ways to measure out what is needed.

1. Cut the pound into the required amount. One pound of butter is 2 cups. Suppose your recipe calls for 1/2 cup. Simply mark the surface of the pound of butter at the half-way point, to indicate two one-cup portions. Cut one of those portions in half and you will have 1/2 cup.

2. Submerge pieces of hard butter in a measuring cup with cold water. This can be a useful technique when you are starting with less than a full pound. Suppose you need 1/4 cup. Fill a glass measuring cup with cold water to the 1/2 cup line, add chunks of butter, being sure they are completely submerged, until water rises to the 3/4 cup line. Drain off the water, and you are left with 1/4 cup butter.

How Much in a Package?

We are including this chart for Angela, who asked the question, and anyone else who would find it helpful to know. It is especially useful for those who buy in bulk. Recipes often call for a particular size of package—for example, a 170 g package of chocolate chips. Now you'll know that you need to measure out 1 cup from your bulk supplies.

	Package size	Imperial	Metric

Almonds,
    flaked
    slivered
	100 g
	100 g
		1 1/4 cups
		1 cup
			300 mL
			250 mL

Apple	1 medium, diced	1 cup	250 mL
Apricots, dried	250 g, cut up	1 1/3 cups	325 mL
Butter	1 lb./454 g	2 cups	500 mL
Butterscotch chips	300 g 170 g	1 3/4 cups 1 cup	425 mL 250 mL
Candied cherries	225 g	1 cup	250 mL
Chocolate chips	300 g 170 g	1 3/4 cups 1 cup	425 mL 250 mL
Chocolate squares	1 square	1 oz.	28 g
Dates, chopped	1lb./500 g	2 cups	500 mL
Figs, chopped	1 lb./500 g	2 2/3 cups	650 mL
Graham wafer crumbs	14 squares	1 cup	250 mL
Icing sugar	1 lb./500 g	3 1/2 cups	875 mL
Lemon	1 medium	3 tbsp. juice 2 tsp. peel	50 mL 10 mL
Margarine	1 lb./454 g	2 cups	500 mL
Marshmallows, mini	400 g	9 cups	2 L

Orange
    cut up
    juice
    peel
	1 medium	
		2/3 cup
		1/3 cup
		2 tbsp.
			
			150 mL
			75 mL
			30 mL

Shortening	1 lb./454 g	2 1/3 cup	325 mL
Smarties	125 g	2/3 cup	150 mL
Sweetened condensed milk	1 can	1 1/4 cups	300 mL
Vanilla wafer crumbs	28 wafers	1 cup	250 mL

Cookie-Making Terms

The terms used in cooking instructions have specific meanings but they can be confusing for new cooks. We have written the recipes with care, and to facilitate their easy use we are including the following definitions.

Cream: To make soft, smooth and creamy by beating with a mixer, or a spoon if you have strong arm muscles!

Cut in: To distribute solid fat throughout flour with a pastry blender or two knives used in scissor fashion. This is continued until fat particles are of the desired size.

Drop: To scoop dough with a spoon, making it rounded or heaped depending on the size of cookie desired. Another spoon is used to push dough onto the cookie sheet.

Fold: To combine one ingredient with another very gently to avoid loss of air. The motion consists of cutting vertically through the mixture with a spoon or spatula, sliding across the bottom of the bowl, bringing it up the side, and turning it over. Bowl is turned a quarter-turn and the process repeated until ingredients are just blended. Proper folding may be a key to recipe success.

Kneading lightly: To gently work dough with hands by folding it over onto itself, then pushing down and away with heels of hands. The dough is turned one-quarter turn after each folding/pushing motion.

Roll out: To lightly roll dough to required thickness, working from the centre out to maintain uniform thickness.

Rub in: To mix fat with flour, using fingers, until mixture has the texture of bread crumbs.

Shape: To use hands to roll or mould dough into balls, rolls or other desired forms.

Sieve: To remove lumps from flour or icing sugar by pushing it through a sieve, using the back of a spoon.

Types of Cookies

Drop cookies are popular because they are quick to prepare, as the dough is simply dropped from a spoon onto the cookie sheet. Drop cookie dough is usually similar to cake dough, but stiffer.

Rolled cookies are made from a stiffer dough that can be shaped into a large ball and rolled out with a rolling pin. Dough for rolled cookies should usually be stiff but not dry. If it is difficult to handle, chilling in the refrigerator for 1-3 hours usually resolves the problem. If dough is too sticky to handle, working in more flour may make it more manageable. Cookies should be rolled on a lightly floured surface. If too much flour is worked into the dough during the rolling stage, the cookies become tough. The thinner the dough is rolled, the shorter the baking time and the crisper the cookie will be.

Shaped and formed cookies are made from dough that is soft but not sticky. Most often it is rolled into balls rather than dropped from a spoon. Sometimes the dough is left as-is, sometimes the ball is flattened with a fork, your fingers, or the bottom of a glass. Whether or not the dough needs to be flattened depends on the proportion of ingredients. Recipe instructions indicate whether or not to flatten the dough. Cookies made with a cookie press also fall in this category.

Refrigerator cookies are made from a shapeable dough that is formed into rolls which are refrigerated for several hours or overnight. They are then sliced and baked. The rolls can be refrigerated for up to a week or kept in the freezer for longer storage. Refrigerator cookies are appealing when one wants fresh-baked cookies without having to mix dough each time.

Unbaked cookies are often simple to make and may contain fewer ingredients. Another appeal, of course, is that the oven need not be turned on.

Bar cookies, in their simplest form, are made from cookie dough which is pressed into a pan, baked, and cut into bars. More elaborate versions are made of bases with a filling layer, and sometimes an icing. Some seem more like cakes than cookies, but because they are all so good, we decided to include them in this book.

Using a Food Processor When Making Cookies and Bars

People who are accustomed to using a food processor find it convenient for the preparation of cookies and bars. We have included one recipe written specifically for the food processor, but others in this book could be adapted. The following guidelines give general directions for adapting recipes. Some techniques may vary with different brands, so check your machine's manual.

Preparation:
- Generally the steel blade is used. On some machines, the plastic blade is specifically designed for doughs. Check your manual.
- Process dry foods before wet ones when possible. That way, you'll need to wash the work bowl only once.
- Butter or margarine used in doughs should be very cold or even frozen. When it is at room temperature, it tends to melt during processing, causing the cookies to be heavy.
- Avoid over-processing once flour is added, as this will make cookies tough.
- Using an on/off or pulse technique prevents over-blending of the flour. If machine does not have an automatic pulse setting, turn it on and off manually, leaving machine on for about 1 second each time. Continue until desired consistency or texture is achieved.
- Do not process cookie dough that calls for more than 2 1/2 cups (625 mL) flour unless the operating manual specifies that your machine can use larger amounts. Some references suggest dividing larger recipes in half and processing in two batches.

To make cookies or single-layer bars:
- Process sugar and ice-cold butter until fluffy.
- Add eggs, flavourings and leavening; process until just mixed.
- Add flour, processing very briefly with an on/off technique until just combined.
- Add any nuts, raisins or chocolate chips last, mixing very briefly with on/off technique.

To make layered bars:

- Use on/off technique to process flour, sugar and ice-cold butter until mixture resembles coarse crumbs. Press into pan and bake, where required.
- Using the same work bowl to prepare filling, process eggs, sugar and flavourings until just blended.
- Stir in fruit, nuts or chocolate chips last, mixing very briefly with on/off technique.

To make graham or vanilla wafer crumbs:

- Use steel blade.
- Place up to 2 cups (500 mL) broken wafers in work bowl.
- Process until crumbs are of desired texture.

Sources:
Food Processor Cuisine by Bonnie Stern
Food Processor Techniques by the Editors of Consumer Guide

Food Processor Shortbread

2 cups	all-purpose flour	500 mL
1/2 cup	berry sugar	125 mL
1 cup	cold butter, cut into 8 cubes	250 mL

Preheat oven to 300°F (150°C).

Measure flour and sugar into food processor bowl. Process for a few seconds to mix. Add butter. Process on/off for 30 seconds or until mixture forms fine crumbs. Stir through with a fork to make sure no large lumps of butter remain. Process for 20 seconds longer or until dough starts to form clumps.

Turn mixture into ungreased 9-inch (22 cm) square baking pan. Press evenly into pan. Pierce all over with tines of a fork. Bake for 50 minutes or until firm and very lightly browned. Cut into small bars or squares while still slightly warm.

Makes about 2 dozen.

Using a Microwave Oven
When Making Cookies and Bars

To soften cream cheese: Remove cheese from packaging and place in a bowl or on a plate. Microwave, uncovered, on medium-low (30%) power at 30-second intervals until desired consistency is reached.

To *soften* butter or margarine: Microwave 1/2 cup (125 mL) on medium-low (30%) power for 20 - 30 seconds, or until desired consistency is achieved.

To *melt* butter or margarine: Place in an oven-proof glass dish or measuring cup. Microwave, covered, on high (100%) power for up to 60 seconds, checking at 10 - 15 second intervals until melted.

To melt 2 chocolate squares: Halve squares; microwave on medium (50%) power for 2 - 3 minutes, stirring at 1-minute intervals. Squares retain their shape until stirred.

To melt chocolate and butterscotch chips: Microwave 1/2 cup (125 mL) on medium (50%) power for 3 - 4 minutes. Chips retain shape until stirred.

To soften brown sugar: Place brown sugar in a casserole dish with a wedge of apple or a slice of bread. Microwave, covered tightly, on high (100%) power for 1 minute. Mash softened sugar with a fork, and continue microwaving at 30-second intervals until soft.

To get more juice from a lemon, lime or orange: Microwave on high (100%) power for 30 seconds.

To toast coconut: Spread 1 1/2 cups (375 mL) coconut in a 9-inch (22 cm) glass pie plate. Microwave, uncovered, on high (100%) power for 6 - 8 minutes or until golden brown, stirring twice. Let stand 5 minutes. Do not attempt to completely brown coconut in the microwave oven as the toasting process continues during standing.

To toast raw sesame seeds: Spread 1/2 cup (125 mL) raw sesame seeds in a 9-inch (22 cm) glass pie plate. Microwave, uncovered, on high (100%) power for 10 - 12 minutes, stirring 2 or 3 times near the end of the toasting time. Watch carefully as the seeds brown quickly during the last 2 minutes, and some toasting continues after removal from the microwave oven.

To toast slivered almonds: Spread 1/2 cup (125 mL) in a 9-inch (22 cm) glass pie plate. Microwave, uncovered, on high (100%) power for 5 - 7 minutes or until almonds are beginning to brown, stirring twice. Let stand for 5 minutes.

To cook date filling: Combine chopped dates and water in a 1 - 2 quart (1 - 2 L) casserole dish. Use less water than recommended in the recipe because less evaporation occurs when cooking in the microwave oven. Microwave, uncovered, on high (100%) power, stirring every 2 minutes until date mixture is bubbling and thickened. 2 cups (500 mL) chopped dates with 1 cup (250 mL) water takes 4 - 6 minutes.

To cook sugar/syrup/butter mixtures: Use large deep microwave-safe dish or casserole that is more than double the volume of the ingredients; this will accomodate the increase in volume that occurs during boiling. Microwave, uncovered, on high (100%) power until ingredients begin to boil, stirring once or twice. Reduce power to medium-low (30%) to maintain a gentle boil. Stir occasionally to dissolve the sugar. Continue cooking until desired temperature or time is reached. Boiling time will be the same as specified in the recipe.

To make lemon butter: In a 4-cup (1 L) glass measure, stir together eggs and sugar until thoroughly mixed. Stir in lemon juice, peel and butter, if called for in recipe. Microwave, uncovered, on medium (50%) power for 10 - 15 minutes, or until mixture bubbles, stirring every 2 minutes.

Baking cookies in a microwave oven:
Most people use the conventional oven for cookies because more can be baked at a time. However, small numbers of cookies can be baked in the microwave oven if it has an even cooking pattern.

To microwave cookies, arrange 6 - 9 cookies in a circle on wax paper, parchment paper or a microwave cookie tray. Microwave on medium to medium-high (50 - 70%) power for 2 - 3 minutes, rotating paper or tray at least once. When done, cookie surfaces will appear dry.

Making bars in a microwave oven:

Some bar recipes can be made in a microwave oven. When adapting recipes, be prepared to experiment, and watch the food carefully. In general, microwave *timing* is about one-quarter of conventional cooking time. Calculate what that would be, then do your first check half-way through your estimated time. For example, if a bar base takes 20 minutes in a conventional oven, estimate the microwave time at 5 minutes, and begin checking after 2 1/2 minutes.

Always *use potholders* to remove baking dishes. Ingredients such as sugar, butter and syrup get very hot; their heat transfers to the baking dish, making it too hot to handle with bare hands.

A round *baking dish* cooks most evenly. Square or rectangular ones often result in corners that are overcooked by the time the centre is done. To prevent this, corners can be shielded with small triangles of aluminum foil for the last few minutes of cooking.

For even cooking, rotate the baking dish once or twice.

Many squares are made up of two or more *layers*. Pre-cook the first layer on medium (50%) power for best results. The next layer can be partially cooked in a separate bowl before spreading it on the base. Both layers can then be cooked together, if necessary.

Marshmallow Crispies

1/4 cup	butter or margarine*	50	mL
15	marshmallows (regular size)	15	
1/2 tsp.	vanilla	2	mL
3 1/2 cups	crispy rice cereal	875	mL

In a large bowl, microwave butter on high (100%) power for 30 - 60 seconds or until melted. Add marshmallows, tossing to coat with butter. Microwave, covered with wax paper, on high (100%) power for 1 - 2 minutes or until smooth when stirred; stir after 30 seconds. Blend in vanilla. Stir in cereal, mixing until evenly coated. Press into a lightly-greased 8-inch (20 cm) square baking dish.

Makes about 2 dozen.

* Use solid margarine; see page 4 for explanation.

Celebration
Cookies

Dropped

Shaped

Rolled

Refrigerator

Unbaked

Bars

Celebration Cookies

1. Almond Shortcake *p. 19*
2. Festive Fruitcake Cookies *p. 20*
3. Lace Cookies *p. 21*
4. Daiquiri Truffles *p. 22*
5. Ginger Shortbread *p. 23*

Almond Shortcake

Attractive — great flavour — an ideal food gift.

3/4 cup	butter, softened	175	mL
1 cup	granulated sugar	250	mL
1/4 cup	almond paste	60	mL
1	egg, beaten	1	
1/2 tsp.	almond flavouring	2	mL
1 tsp.	baking powder	5	mL
1/2 tsp.	salt	2	mL
2 cups	all-purpose flour	500	mL
5	almonds, halved	5	
	(for decoration)		

Preheat oven to 325°F (160°C).

In a medium bowl, cream butter, sugar and almond paste. Mix in half of the egg along with almond flavouring, baking powder and salt. Stir in flour. Knead lightly.

Lightly butter two 8-inch (20 cm) round cake pans or pie plates. Press dough into pans, scoring edge with the tines of a fork. Brush remainder of egg over top. Arrange almond halves in circle on surface of each short-cake. Press into dough. Bake for 25 minutes or until lightly browned. Transfer to racks to cool. Cut into narrow wedges to serve.

Makes two 8-inch (20 cm) shortcakes.

Festive Fruitcake Cookies

Easy, colourful, scrumptious!

1 cup	raisins	250 mL
1 cup	coarsely chopped candied cherries	250 mL
1 cup	coarsely chopped candied pineapple	250 mL
1/2 cup	coarsely chopped Brazil nuts	125 mL
1/2 cup	shortening, softened	125 mL
3/4 cup	granulated sugar	175 mL
1	egg	1
1 tsp.	vanilla	5 mL
1/2 tsp.	almond extract	2 mL
1 cup	all-purpose flour	250 mL
1 tsp.	baking powder	5 mL
1/2 tsp.	salt	2 mL

Preheat oven to 350°F (180°C).

In a medium bowl, combine fruit and nuts.

In a large bowl, cream shortening and sugar. Beat in egg, vanilla and almond extract. On low speed, thoroughly beat in flour, baking powder and salt. Stir in fruit and nuts.

Bake a test cookie; see page 6 for directions.

Drop dough from a teaspoon onto greased cookie sheet. Bake for 10 minutes or until golden. Transfer to racks to cool.

Makes about 3 dozen.

Restoring moisture to candied fruit

Candied cherries, pineapple, citron, and peel may dry out during storage. To restore moisture, place fruit on a steamer rack in a saucepan containing some water. Cover saucepan and steam for about 5 minutes, or until fruit is moist again.

Lace Cookies

This old-time cookie has a marvelous butterscotch flavour
and crisp texture.

1/4 cup	butter	50	mL
	(do not use margarine)		
1/4 cup	brown sugar	50	mL
1/4 cup	corn syrup	50	mL
1/2 cup	all-purpose flour	100	mL
1 tsp.	vanilla	5	mL

Preheat oven to 350°F (180°C).

In a heavy saucepan over medium heat, combine butter, sugar and syrup. Heat, stirring frequently, until sugar dissolves and mixture comes to a boil. Remove from heat. Stir in flour and vanilla. Batter will be thin.

Bake a test cookie; it should spread dramatically to about 3 inches (7 cm) in diameter. See page 6 for directions.

Drop batter from a teaspoon several inches apart onto parchment-lined cookie sheet.* Bake for 8 minutes or until golden in colour. Let stand about 1 minute, then transfer to racks to cool.

Makes 3 - 4 dozen.

Variations:

Dip half of each cookie in melted semi-sweet or white chocolate chips or squares.

Or let stand 30 seconds, then shape around the handle of a wooden spoon or pencil to form a cornucopia. If cookies become too hard to shape, place back in oven briefly to soften.

* Lace cookies can be baked on a greased cookie sheet, but parchment paper gives better results. Because of the high proportions of sugar and syrup to flour, they brown quickly around the edge and tend to stick. Parchment paper promotes even browning and easy removal of baked cookies. It is available in supermarkets.

Cookie pieces contain no calories; they leak out when the cookies are broken.

Daiquiri Truffles

Flavoured crumbs surround a soft chocolate centre.
Our home economist reported:
"Delicious, unusual, a bit more fuss but worth it."

1 cup	chocolate chips, melted	250	mL
1/4 cup	sour cream	50	mL
1	box (250 g) vanilla wafers, made into crumbs	1	
1 cup	icing sugar	250	mL
1 cup	finely-chopped pecans	250	mL
1/4 tsp.	salt	1	mL
3 tbsp.	cocoa	50	mL
1 tbsp.	grated lemon peel	15	mL
1 tbsp.	grated orange peel	15	mL
2 1/2 tbsp.	lemon juice	40	mL
1 1/2 tbsp.	maple syrup or corn syrup	25	mL
1/4 cup	rum*	50	mL
	Icing sugar		

In a small bowl, combine melted chocolate chips and sour cream. Chill for 30 minutes or until mixture can be shaped into balls. Using approximately one teaspoon (5 mL) of mixture, shape into balls 1/2-inch (1 cm) in diameter. Refrigerate while preparing the coating.

In a medium bowl, combine wafer crumbs, icing sugar, pecans, salt, cocoa, lemon peel and orange peel.

In a small bowl, combine lemon juice, syrup and rum. Stir into crumb mixture. Refrigerate briefly for easier handling. Use hands to shape a coating around the chocolate balls; finished daiquiri ball will be about 1 1/2 inches (4 cm) in diameter. Roll in icing sugar. For best flavour, refrigerate 3 days in a covered container before serving.

Makes about 3 dozen.

* Substitute 1/4 cup (50 mL) orange juice and 1/2 teaspoon (2 mL) rum flavouring, if preferred.

Ginger Shortbread

This recipe will be a hit with all who like candied ginger — a good
traditional shortbread without it.

1 cup	butter, softened	250 mL
	(do not use margarine)	
1/2 cup	brown sugar	125 mL
1/2 cup	finely-chopped	125 mL
	candied ginger	
2 cups	all-purpose flour	500 mL

Preheat oven to 350°F (180°C).

In a medium bowl, cream butter thoroughly. Add sugar and beat well.
Stir in ginger, then three-quarters of the flour. Continue adding flour
until dough is firm but not dry and cracked.

On a lightly-floured surface, knead dough gently but thoroughly. Roll
out to 1/2-inch (1 cm) thickness. Cut into small squares and place on
ungreased cookie sheet. Bake for 12 minutes or until light golden colour. Transfer to racks to cool.

Makes 3 - 4 dozen.

Variation:

Press dough into 9 x 13-inch (22 x 34 cm) pan. Bake at 300°F (150°C)
for 20 minutes or until light golden colour. Cut into squares or bars when
still slightly warm.

Make this book yours.

*If the baking time or temperature in your oven varies from what
is specified in our recipes, make a note right on the recipe about
how much it should be adjusted. That way, you'll have the
information you need the next time you make a particular recipe.*

Cream Cheese
Christmas Wreaths

Attractive and tasty — a nice addition to Christmas baking.

1 cup	butter or margarine*, softened	250 mL
1	package (250 g) cream cheese, softened	1
1 cup	granulated sugar	250 mL
1 1/2 tsp.	vanilla	7 mL
2 cups	all-purpose flour	500 mL
	Sliced unblanched almonds	
	Sliced red or green candied cherries	

Preheat oven to 350°F (180°C).

In a large bowl, cream butter, cheese, sugar and vanilla until fluffy. Add flour gradually, beating until thoroughly blended.

Bake a test cookie; see page 6 for directions.

Working with 1 cup (250 mL) at a time, press dough through cookie press or pastry bag fitted with a large star-tip tube onto ungreased cookie sheet to form wreath-shaped or plain round cookies. Garnish with almonds and cherries, to create the effect of Christmas wreaths. Bake for 12 minutes or until browned on edges and bottom. Transfer to racks to cool.

Makes about 6 dozen.

* Use solid margarine; see page 4 for explanation.

Mincemeat or Date Squares

Mincemeat is a tasty alternative to dates. Sprinkling them with sugar helps to differentiate them from date squares — a plus for those who don't like surprises.

1 1/2 cups	all-purpose or whole wheat flour	375 mL
1/2 cup	brown sugar	125 mL
1/2 cup	rolled oats	125 mL
3/4 cup	butter or margarine*	175 mL
1 cup	mincemeat**	250 mL
	Icing sugar (optional)	

Preheat oven to 350°F (180°C).

In a medium bowl, combine flour, sugar and rolled oats. Using a pastry blender or two knives, cut in butter until mixture resembles coarse crumbs. Press two-thirds of crumbs into ungreased 9-inch (22 cm) square baking pan.

Process mincemeat in blender or food processor until smooth. Pour over bottom layer of crumbs. Sprinkle reserved crumbs over mincemeat. Press gently. Bake for 25 minutes or until set and golden brown. Dust lightly with icing sugar when cool.

Makes about 3 dozen.

* Use solid margarine; see page 4 for explanation.
** To make date squares, substitute date filling recipe on page 77. Omit the icing sugar.

Children's Cottage — love in action

Children's Cottage is a crisis nursery providing a safe, cheerful and home-like environment for babies and preschool children in any family emergency. When no other care is available, parents may leave their children while the problem is being resolved. No fee is charged for this service.

Cranberry Orange Drops

Chewy, with a tangy citrus flavour.

1/2 cup	butter or margarine*, softened	125	mL
1 cup	brown sugar	250	mL
1	egg	1	
1 tsp.	finely grated orange peel	5	mL
1 tsp.	baking powder	5	mL
1/2 tsp.	ground allspice	2	mL
1 cup	all-purpose flour	250	mL
2 cups	rolled oats	500	mL
1 cup	whole cranberry sauce Orange Glaze	250	mL

Preheat oven to 375°F (190°C).

In a medium bowl, cream butter, brown sugar, egg, orange peel, baking powder and allspice.

Blend in flour. Stir in rolled oats and cranberry sauce.

Bake a test cookie; see page 6 for directions.

Drop batter from a teaspoon onto lightly greased cookie sheet. Bake for 10 minutes or until lightly browned. Transfer to racks to cool. Drizzle glaze over cookies while still warm.

Orange Glaze

1 cup	icing sugar	250	mL
1 tsp.	grated orange peel	5	mL
2 tbsp.	orange juice	25	mL

In a small bowl, thoroughly combine ingredients.

Makes about 3 dozen.

* Use solid margarine; see page 4 for explanation.

Lebkuchen

These spicy bars are ideal for mailing — they keep well and the flavour improves with age. Dough requires overnight chilling.

3/4 cup	liquid honey	175	mL
3/4 cup	dark brown sugar	175	mL
2 tbsp.	butter	30	mL
1	egg	1	
	Grated peel of one orange		
1/2 tsp.	baking soda	2	mL
1/2 tsp.	salt	2	mL
2 tsp.	ground nutmeg	10	mL
2 tsp.	ground ginger	10	mL
1 tsp.	ground cinnamon	5	mL
1 tsp.	ground allspice	5	mL
2 1/2 cups	all-purpose flour	625	mL
3/4 cup	chopped candied fruit	175	mL
3/4 cup	slivered almonds, finely chopped	175	mL
	Glaze		

In a large saucepan, heat honey, sugar and butter. Cook and stir until sugar has dissolved and butter melted. Do not boil. Cool to room temperature. Stir in egg, orange peel, baking soda, salt and spices. Stir in about three-quarters of the flour. Continue adding flour until dough is stiff. Mix in fruit and nuts. Cover and chill at least overnight. If time permits, leave three days for maximum blending of flavours.

Preheat oven to 350°F (180°C).

On a lightly floured surface, working with one-quarter of the dough at a time, roll a rectangle 1/2-inch (1 cm) thick. Cut into bars 1 x 2 1/2 inches (2.5 x 7 cm). Place on lightly greased cookie sheet. Bake for 10 minutes or until dry on top and golden brown on bottom. Transfer to cooling racks and spread with glaze while still warm.

Glaze

1 cup	icing sugar	250	mL
2 tbsp.	hot water	25	mL

In a small bowl, stir icing sugar and water until smooth.

Makes 3 - 4 dozen.

Coconut Sugar Cookies

Dee-licious!
Dough requires chilling for 3 hours.

1 cup	butter, softened	250	mL
1 cup	granulated sugar	250	mL
1/2 tsp.	salt	2	mL
1	egg	1	
1 cup	finely-shredded coconut	250	mL
2 cups	all-purpose flour	500	mL
	Glaze		

In a medium bowl, cream butter, sugar and salt. Add egg and beat well. Stir in coconut. Blend in about three-quarters of the flour. Continue adding flour until dough is soft but not sticky. Chill for 3 hours.

Preheat oven to 350°F (180°C).

On a floured surface, roll half the dough to a thickness of 1/16-inch (2 mm). Chill remainder until ready to use. Cut rolled dough with cookie cutter and place on ungreased cookie sheet. Bake for 10 minutes or until light golden brown. Glaze and transfer to racks to cool.

Glaze

3/4 cup	icing sugar	175	mL
4 tsp.	water or lemon juice	25	mL

In a small bowl, combine icing sugar and water or lemon juice. Glaze should be thin but spreadable. Add more icing sugar or water to adjust consistency as necessary.

Makes about 5 dozen.

Other Sugar Cookie Recipes in this Book

The above recipes are for cookies that are rolled and cut. For a quicker version of sugar cookies, see

---

Oatmeal Shortbread

A delicious variation of an old-time favourite.

1 cup	butter, softened (do not use margarine)	250	mL
3/4 cup	granulated sugar	175	mL
3/4 tsp.	salt	4	mL
1 1/2 cups	all-purpose flour	375	mL
1 1/2 cups	rolled oats	375	mL

Preheat oven to 325°F (160°C).

In a medium bowl, cream butter and sugar. Gradually stir in salt, flour and oats, blending well. Press into 9 x 13-inch (22 x 34 cm) baking pan. Bake for 30 minutes or until a light golden colour.

Makes 4 - 5 dozen.

Holiday Cut-Outs

An easy recipe that lends itself to decorating, but is
just as good plain.
Dough requires chilling for at least 3 hours.

1 cup	butter, softened	250 mL
2/3 cup	granulated sugar	150 mL
1	egg	1
1 tsp.	vanilla	5 mL
1/2 tsp.	salt	2 mL
2 1/2 cups	all-purpose flour	625 mL

In a large bowl, cream butter and sugar. Beat in egg, vanilla, and salt. Stir in flour, a third at a time, mixing well. Add last third of the flour gradually, stopping when rolling consistency has been achieved. Cover dough with wax paper or plastic, and chill for at least 3 hours.

Preheat oven to 350°F (180°C).

On a lightly floured surface, working with half the dough at a time, roll to 1/8 inch (3 mm) thickness. With lightly floured cookie cutter, cut dough into desired shapes. If dough becomes difficult to handle, chill it again. Place cookies on ungreased cookie sheet. Bake for 10 minutes or until golden. Transfer to racks to cool. May be iced if desired.

Makes about 6 dozen.

Cookies can be ornaments to hang on the Christmas tree. To create a loop for hanging them, cut string in 3-inch pieces, fold each piece in half, and press the cut ends into the underside of unbaked cookies. The finished cookies will have loops baked right into them.

Mincemeat Refrigerator Cookies

Lightly spiced — very good.
Dough requires overnight chilling.

1/2 cup	shortening	125 mL
1/4 cup	butter	50 mL
1 cup	sugar	250 mL
1	egg	1
1/8 tsp.	almond extract	0.5 mL
1 tsp.	grated lemon peel	5 mL
1/2 tsp.	baking soda	2 mL
1/2 tsp.	salt	2 mL
1/2 tsp.	ground cinnamon	2 mL
1/2 tsp.	ground mace	2 mL
2 1/2 cups	all-purpose flour	625 mL
1/2 cup	mincemeat	125 mL
1/4 cup	finely chopped Brazil nuts	50 mL

In a medium bowl, cream shortening and butter. Cream in sugar until light and fluffy. Beat in egg, almond extract, lemon peel, baking soda, salt and spices. Stir flour into creamed mixture alternately with mincemeat. Mix in nuts. Shape into rolls 1 1/2-inches (4 cm) in diameter. Wrap in plastic or wax paper. Chill overnight.

Preheat oven to 375°F (190°C).

With a thin sharp knife, slice cookies 1/4-inch (6 mm) thick. Place on ungreased cookie sheet. Bake for 12 minutes or until lightly browned. Transfer to racks to cool.

Makes 4 - 5 dozen.

Cutting Refrigerator Cookies

When using a knife, it must be thin and sharp to cut the cookies without squashing the roll as it slices. A speedy alternative is to use unflavoured dental floss or heavy thread. Use a piece about one foot long. Place under roll of dough, bring ends over top, cross them and pull firmly.

Crunchy Peanut Butter Logs

A crunchy coating surrounds a creamy peanut butter filling
in this unbaked dainty.

1 cup	smooth peanut butter	250	mL
1 cup	icing sugar	250	mL
1 1/4 cups	finely crushed bran flakes, divided	300	mL
1/3 cup	finely-chopped pecans or walnuts	75	mL
1/3 cup	fine coconut	75	mL
3 tbsp.	melted butter	50	mL
2 tbsp.	molasses	25	mL

In a medium bowl, cream peanut butter and icing sugar. Shape into four logs, each 6 inches (15 cm) in length.

In another bowl, combine 3/4 cup (175 mL) bran flakes, nuts, coconut, butter and molasses. Press around logs. Roll logs in remaining bran flakes. Wrap in plastic and store in refrigerator or freezer. To serve, cut into 1/2-inch (1 cm) slices.

Makes about 4 dozen.

Ginger Sparkles

An old favourite at Christmas or any time of the year.

3/4 cup	butter or margarine*, softened	175 mL
1 cup	granulated sugar	250 mL
1	egg	1
1/4 cup	molasses	50 mL
2 tsp.	baking soda	10 mL
1/2 tsp.	salt	2 mL
1 1/4 tsp.	ground ginger	7 mL
1 tsp.	ground cinnamon	5 mL
2 cups	all-purpose or whole wheat flour	500 mL
	Granulated sugar	

Preheat oven to 350°F (180°C).

In a medium bowl, cream butter and sugar. Beat in egg, then molasses, baking soda, salt and spices. Stir in flour.

Bake a test cookie; see page 6 for directions.

Shape dough into 1-inch (2.5 cm) balls. Shake, a few at a time, in bag with small amount of granulated sugar. Place on lightly greased cookie sheet. Bake for 10 minutes or until lightly browned on bottom. Transfer to racks to cool.

Makes about 5 dozen.

* Use solid margarine; see page 4 for explanation.

Peppermint Brownies

Luscious, rich, delightful!

1/2 cup	butter or margarine*	125	mL
3	squares unsweetened chocolate	3	
1 1/4 cups	granulated sugar	300	mL
1/2 tsp.	peppermint extract	2	mL
3	eggs	3	
2/3 cup	all-purpose flour	150	mL
1/2 tsp.	baking powder	2	mL
1/2 tsp.	salt	2	mL
1/2 cup	chopped almonds	125	mL
	Peppermint Icing		

Preheat oven to 350°F (180°C).

In a heavy saucepan over low heat, melt butter and chocolate, stirring until smooth. Remove from heat. Add sugar, peppermint extract and eggs; beat well.

In a small bowl, combine flour, baking powder, salt and almonds. Add to chocolate mixture, stirring until well blended. Spread in a greased 9-inch (22 cm) square baking pan. Bake for 25 minutes or until top springs back when touched lightly and sides have begun to pull away from pan. Cool. Frost with Peppermint Icing.

Peppermint Icing

3 tbsp.	butter or margarine, softened and divided	50	mL
1 tbsp.	whipping or cereal cream	15	mL
	Red food colouring		
1 tsp.	peppermint extract	5	mL
1 cup	icing sugar	250	mL
1	square unsweetened chocolate	1	

In a small bowl, combine 2 tablespoons butter, cream, a few drops of food colouring, peppermint extract and icing sugar. Spread over brownies. Refrigerate 5 minutes. Melt chocolate and remaining butter, stirring to combine. Drizzle over frosting.

Makes about 2 dozen.

* Use solid margarine; see page 4 for explanation.

Almond Crescents

An attractive and tasty special-occasion cookie.

1 cup	butter, softened	250	mL
	(do not use margarine)		
1/4 cup	icing sugar	60	mL
1 tbsp.	water	15	mL
2 tsp.	vanilla	10	mL
1/4 tsp.	salt	1	mL
2 cups	all-purpose flour	500	mL
1 cup	chopped almonds	250	mL
	Icing sugar (optional)		

Preheat oven to 325°F (160°C).

In a large bowl, cream butter, icing sugar, water, vanilla and salt. Stir in flour, then almonds.

Bake a test cookie; see page 6 for directions.

Roll into pieces the size of an index finger. Place on ungreased cookie sheet, forming each roll into a crescent shape. Bake for 20 minutes or until barely browned on bottom. Transfer to racks to cool. Sprinkle with icing sugar, if desired.

Makes 3 - 4 dozen.

Variation:

Dip ends of cooled cookies in melted semisweet chocolate.

From a 1905 Cookbook — for your consideration:

"Many mishaps occur from a lack of forethought. Do not begin to make a dish until you have carefully read over the recipe, collected all the ingredients, and fixed the fire. Do one thing at a time. Make haste without hurrying. Cakes, pastry and such delicate dishes should be made when there is no other cooking going on in the kitchen. Give them your whole time."

Lemon Strips

Dee-licious!

1/2 cup	butter, softened	125	mL
1 1/4 cup	granulated sugar, divided	300	mL
1/4 tsp.	ground ginger (optional)	1	mL
1 2/3 cups	graham wafer crumbs	400	mL
1/3 cup	all-purpose flour	75	mL
3	egg yolks	3	
1 tbsp.	water	15	mL
1/4 cup	lemon juice	50	mL
	Grated peel of 1 lemon		

Preheat oven to 325°F (160°C).

In a medium bowl, cream butter, 1/2 cup (125 mL) sugar and ginger. Stir in crumbs. Press about two-thirds of mixture evenly in an ungreased 9-inch (22 cm) square baking pan. Bake for 5 minutes. Let stand on cooling rack while preparing filling.

Increase oven temperature to 350°F (180°C).

In top of double boiler*, combine remaining 3/4 cup (175 mL) sugar, flour, egg yolks, water, lemon juice and peel. Cook, stirring frequently, for 15 minutes or until thickened. Pour over crust and spread evenly. Cover with remaining crumbs. Smooth top and press lightly. Bake for 20 minutes or until lightly browned. Let stand to mellow for 12 hours or more. Cut into narrow strips to serve.

Makes about 2 dozen.

* If not available, use a heavy saucepan over low heat.

Nut drops: A quick and tasty way to use leftover egg white.

> *1 egg white*
> *1 cup (250 mL) brown sugar*
> *1 package (100 g) pecan pieces*

In a deep small bowl, beat egg white until stiff. Beat in sugar; stir in nuts. Drop small spoonfuls onto greased cookie sheets, allowing room for spreading. Bake at 300°F (150°C) for 20 minutes or until browned. Makes about 2 dozen.

Children's Cottage Cookie Cook Book

Chocolate Caramel Shortcake Bars

Luscious!

1 cup	all-purpose flour	250	mL
1/4 cup	granulated sugar	50	mL
1 cup	butter, divided	250	mL
1/2 cup	brown sugar	125	mL
1/2 cup	sweetened condensed milk	125	mL
2 tbsp.	corn syrup	30	mL
1	milk chocolate bar (100 g), melted	1	

Preheat oven to 350°F (180°C).

In a medium bowl, combine flour and granulated sugar. Cut in 1/2 cup (125 mL) butter until mixture resembles coarse crumbs. Press into ungreased 9-inch (22 cm) square baking pan. Bake for 15 minutes or until beginning to brown.

In a heavy saucepan, combine remaining 1/2 cup (125 mL) butter, brown sugar, milk and corn syrup. Cook and stir over medium heat until mixture comes to a boil. Cook, stirring continuously, for 3 minutes more. Pour hot mixture over cooked base. Cool slightly, then refrigerate for 15 minutes or until set. Spread melted chocolate over caramel. Refrigerate 30 minutes or until set.

Makes about 2 dozen.

Variation:

If dark chocolate is preferred, use 2/3 cup (150 mL) chocolate chips in place of the chocolate bar.

Biscotti

This traditional Italian treat is intended for dunking
in cappuccino or sweet red wine, but we think it is also
perfect with tea, hot chocolate, or without being dunked at all!
Biscotti are somewhat finger-like in shape,
crisp in texture and wonderfully flavoured.

1/2 cup	slivered almonds	125 mL
3/4 cup	butter, softened	175 mL
3/4 cup	granulated sugar	175 mL
2	eggs	2
1 1/2 tsp.	baking powder	7 mL
1/4 tsp.	salt	1 mL
1 1/2 tsp.	anise seed	7 mL
3/4 tsp.	almond extract	3 mL
1/2 tsp.	grated orange or lemon peel	2 mL
3 cups	all-purpose flour	750 mL

Preheat oven to 350°F (180°C).

Spread almonds in single layer in shallow pan. Bake in oven for 8 minutes or until nicely toasted. Cool and chop coarsely.

Reduce oven to 325°F (160°C).

In a medium bowl, cream butter and sugar. Beat in eggs, baking powder and salt. Stir in anise seed, almond extract and peel. Blend in about three-quarters of the flour. Stir in almonds. Continue adding flour until dough is soft but not sticky, and can be shaped into a roll.

Divide dough in half. On a lightly-floured surface, form each half into a roll about 13 inches (33 cm) long and 1 1/2 inches (4 cm) in diameter. Place on ungreased cookie sheet at least 4 inches (10 cm) apart. Bake for 25 minutes or until golden brown. Transfer to racks to cool for 5 minutes.

Cut diagonally into 1/2-inch (1 cm) slices. Lay slices flat on cookie sheet and return to oven for 15 minutes or more to dry out, turning slices over after 5 minutes. Transfer to racks to cool. Store in tightly covered container.

Makes about 3 dozen.

Variation:
Chocolate Biscotti: Omit anise seed and peel. Reduce flour to 2 1/2 cups (625 mL) and add 1/2 cup (125 mL) cocoa along with the flour.

Children's Cottage Cookie Cook Book

Almond-Spice Slices

This is a spicy, tasty recipe which makes an excellent
accompaniment for tea or coffee. Dough requires chilling.

1 cup	butter, softened	250	mL
1 cup	brown sugar	250	mL
2 tbsp.	molasses	30	mL
1	egg	1	
2 tsp.	ground cinnamon	10	mL
1 tsp.	ground ginger*	5	mL
1 tsp.	ground cardamom*	5	mL
1/4 tsp.	salt	1	mL
1 tsp.	baking soda	5	mL
1 cup	coarsely chopped blanched almonds	250	mL
3 cups	all-purpose flour	750	mL

In a large bowl, cream butter, sugar and molasses until light and fluffy.
Beat in egg, spices, salt and baking soda. Stir in almonds. Stir in about
three-quarters of the flour. Continue adding flour to make a stiff dough.

On a lightly floured surface, knead dough until smooth. Divide in half.
Shape each piece into a roll 7 inches (18 cm) long. Flatten each roll into
a rectangle 7 x 3 inches (18 x 7 cm). Wrap in plastic or wax paper. Chill
several hours or overnight.

Preheat oven to 325°F (160°C).

With a thin sharp knife, cut in 1/8-inch (3 mm) slices. Place on lightly
greased cookie sheet. Bake for 10 minutes or until very lightly browned.

Makes about 4 dozen (large).

Variation:

For a Christmas cookie plate, shape into smaller rolls (7 x 1 1/2 inches/
18 x 4 cm). Roll each log in red or green sugar. Proceed as directed.

* If desired, substitute spices of your choice for the ginger and cardamom—for
example nutmeg, cloves, mace or allspice.

Chocolate Crackles

Very good, and easy to make.

3/4 cup	shortening, softened	175	mL
1/4 cup	corn syrup	60	mL
1	egg	1	
1 cup	brown sugar, packed	250	mL
1/4 cup	cocoa	60	mL
1 1/2 tsp	baking soda	7	mL
1/2 tsp	salt	2	mL
2 cups	all-purpose flour	500	mL
	Granulated sugar		

Preheat oven to 350°F (180°C).

In a large bowl, cream shortening and corn syrup. Beat in egg. Blend in sugar, cocoa, baking soda and salt. Stir in flour.

Bake a test cookie; see page 6 for directions.

Roll dough into 1-inch (2.5 cm) balls and shake a few at a time in a bag with a little granulated sugar. Place on ungreased cookie sheet. Bake for 12 minutes or until cookies feel set and tops crack. Transfer to racks to cool.

Makes about 4 dozen.

Coating cookies with sugar

Some recipes call for shaping cookies in balls and rolling in sugar. A quick way to do this is to place some sugar in a small bag, then add 5 or 6 cookies at a time and give them a few shakes. They will be evenly coated in no time.

Date Cherry Cookies

Great flavour!

1 cup	butter or margarine*, softened	250 mL
3/4 cup	granulated sugar	175 mL
3/4 cup	brown sugar	175 mL
2	eggs	2
2 1/2 cups	all-purpose flour	625 mL
1 tsp.	baking soda	5 mL
1 tsp.	cream of tartar	5 mL
1/2 tsp.	salt	2 mL
1/2 cup	chopped dates	125 mL
1/2 cup	drained and chopped maraschino cherries	125 mL
1 cup	fine sweetened coconut	250 mL

Preheat oven to 350°F (180°C).

In a large bowl, cream butter and sugars. Beat in eggs.

In another bowl, combine remaining ingredients. Blend into creamed mixture.

Bake a test cookie; see page 6 for directions.

Drop batter from a teaspoon onto greased cookie sheet. Bake for 12 minutes or until lightly browned. Transfer to racks to cool.

Makes 3 - 4 dozen.

* Use solid margarine; see page 4 for explanation.

From a 1932 Cookbook — Some good advice:

"Unless otherwise suggested, cookies which are dropped from a spoon require a batter stiff enough to hold its shape. In most cases fruits such as raisins, dates or currants may be interchanged or used in various combinations."

Come Again Cookie

Nice addition to a Christmas cookie plate.

1 cup	butter or margarine*, softened	250	mL
1 cup	brown sugar	250	mL
1/2 cup	granulated sugar	125	mL
2	eggs	2	
2 tsp.	vanilla	10	mL
1 tsp.	cream of tartar	5	mL
1 tsp.	baking soda	5	mL
1 cup	raisins	250	mL
1/2 cup	chopped nuts	125	mL
1	package (450 g) mixed candied fruit, finely cut	1	
2 1/4 cups	all-purpose flour	550	mL

Preheat oven to 350°F (180°C).

In a medium bowl, cream butter and sugars. Beat in eggs, vanilla, cream of tartar and baking soda. In a large bowl, combine raisins, nuts, fruit, and 1 cup (250 mL) of the flour. Add creamed mixture and stir thoroughly. Mix in remaining flour.

Bake a test cookie; see page 6 for directions.

Drop dough from a teaspoon onto greased cookie sheet. Bake 12 minutes or until lightly browned. Transfer to racks to cool.

Makes about 5 dozen.

* Use solid margarine; see page 4 for explanation.

If cookies are flattened before baking, they will be more uniform in shape than if they are allowed to spread naturally.

Spanish Peanut Slice

Rich and easy; needs to stand overnight before cutting.

1 1/2 cups	all-purpose flour	375 mL
1/2 cup	brown sugar	125 mL
3/4 cup	butter or margarine*	175 mL
3/4 cup	corn syrup	175 mL
1	package (300 g) butterscotch chips	1
2 tbsp.	vegetable oil	25 mL
1 tbsp.	water	15 mL
2 cups	Spanish peanuts	500 mL

Preheat oven to 350°F (180°C).

In a medium bowl, combine flour and sugar. Using a pastry blender or two knives, cut in butter until mixture resembles coarse crumbs. Press into 9 x 13-inch (22 x 34 cm) pan. Bake for 20 minutes or until golden brown. Cool.

In a heavy saucepan over medium heat, combine syrup, butterscotch chips, oil and water. Cook and stir until melted. Stir in peanuts. Pour over cooked cooled base. Let stand overnight, uncovered, before slicing.

Makes about 4 dozen.

* Use solid margarine; see page 4 for explanation.

Chocolate Brandy Balls

An excellent unbaked goodie.
Pack in small paper or foil candy cups to create
a wonderful Christmas gift from the kitchen.

1 cup	chocolate chips, melted	250 mL
3 tbsp.	corn syrup	50 mL
1/2 cup	brandy or ginger ale	125 mL
2 1/4 cups	crushed chocolate wafers	550 mL
1 cup	finely chopped nuts	250 mL
1/2 cup	icing sugar	125 mL
1/2 cup	finely chopped candied red cherries	125 mL
	Granulated sugar	

In a small bowl, combine chocolate chips, corn syrup and brandy or ginger ale.

In a large bowl, thoroughly combine wafer crumbs, nuts, icing sugar and cherries. Add chocolate mixture and stir until blended. Let stand 30 minutes.

Shape into 1-inch (2.5 cm) balls and roll in granulated sugar. Store in a covered container. These cookies are best left for a day or two, for the flavours to blend and mellow.

Makes 4 - 5 dozen.

Variation:

Red granulated sugar can be used for an especially festive appearance.

 The calories in food used for medicinal purposes never count. This applies especially to cookies such as San Francisco Fudge Foggies, Daiquiri Truffles and Chocolate Brandy Balls.

Rum Balls

Popular at Christmas or any time of the year — attractive on a
tea plate. Requires overnight chilling.

6	squares semi-sweet chocolate	6	
1/2 cup	sour cream	125	mL
1/4 cup	butter, softened	60	mL
1/4 cup	cocoa	60	mL
1/2 tsp.	salt	2	mL
1/4 cup	rum*	60	mL
1 cup	finely chopped pecans	250	mL
2 cups	crushed vanilla wafers	500	mL
1	package (160 g) chocolate sprinkles	1	

In top of double boiler, or in medium bowl set over hot water, melt chocolate and sour cream, stirring until combined. Cool.

Stir in butter, then cocoa and salt. Blend in rum. Add pecans and wafer crumbs, stirring thoroughly. Cover and refrigerate 4 hours or overnight.

With buttered hands, shape mixture into 1-inch (2.5 cm) balls. Roll in chocolate sprinkles. Store in refrigerator. Flavour improves with aging.

Makes about 4 dozen.

* Substitute 3 tablespoons (50 mL) water and 1 teaspoon (5 mL) or more rum flavouring.

Variation:

To make Chocolate Almond Balls, substitute almond-flavoured liqueur for the rum, and ground almonds for the pecans.

Children's Cottage — love in action

Children are cared for at the Cottage for up to three days. This time limit was chosen because it is the length of time children can be separated from their parents without acute anxiety.

Fruit Shortbread

With a roll of this dough in the refrigerator,
you can have freshly baked holiday cookies on short notice.
Dough requires chilling for 2 hours.

1 cup	butter, softened	250 mL
3/4 cup	icing sugar	175 mL
1	egg	1
1 tsp.	vanilla	5 mL
2 1/4 cups	all-purpose flour	550 mL
1/2 cup	drained and chopped maraschino cherries	125 mL
1/2 cup	mixed peel	125 mL

In a medium bowl, cream butter and sugar until fluffy. Beat in egg and vanilla. Blend in about three-quarters of the flour. Continue adding flour until dough is firm but not dry. Stir in cherries and peel.

On a lightly floured surface, form dough into two 8-inch (20 cm) rolls about 1 1/2 inches (4 cm) in diameter. Wrap well and refrigerate at least 2 hours or until rolls are firm enough to slice.

Preheat oven to 350°F (180°C).

With a thin sharp knife, cut into 1/4 inch (6 mm) slices and place on ungreased cookie sheet. Bake for 8 minutes or until slightly golden around edges. Transfer to racks to cool.

Makes about 5 dozen.

Positioning Cookie Sheets

Cookie sheets should be at least 2 inches (5 cm) away from sides of the oven, in order to allow proper circulation of heat.

Hanukkah Cookies

An all-time favourite with children.
Requires chilling.

1/3 cup	butter, softened	75	mL
1 cup	granulated sugar	250	mL
1	egg	1	
1/4 cup	milk	50	mL
1 tsp.	vanilla	5	mL
2 tsp.	baking powder	10	mL
1/2 tsp.	salt	2	mL
2 cups	all-purpose flour	500	mL

In a medium bowl, cream butter. Add sugar, creaming until very smooth. Beat in egg, milk, vanilla, baking powder and salt. Stir in about three-quarters of the flour. Continue adding flour until dough reaches rolling consistency. Chill for 1 hour.

Preheat oven to 350°F (180°C).

On a floured surface, roll dough to a thickness of 1/4 inch (6 mm). Cut into desired shapes using Hanukkah cookie cutters that have been dipped in flour. Place on lightly greased cookie sheet. Bake for 10 minutes or until lightly browned. Transfer to racks to cool. Decorate with coloured sprinkles before baking, or allow cookies to cool and ice with coloured icing.

Makes 2 - 3 dozen.

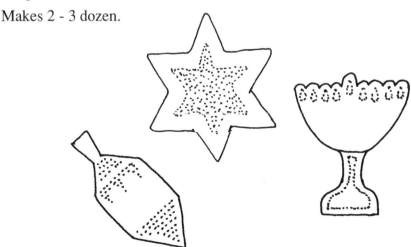

Hamentashen

Hamentashen are one of the traditional foods of Purim,
a Jewish holiday in early March. They are filled cookies
with a triangular shape similar to the tri-cornered hat
worn by Hamen, a chief minister of the Persians;
hence the name "Hamentashen."
Dough requires chilling for at least 3 hours.

1/2 cup	butter or margarine*, softened	125	mL
1/2 cup	granulated sugar	125	mL
1/4 cup	liquid honey	60	mL
1 tsp.	vanilla	5	mL
1 tsp.	vinegar	5	mL
2	eggs	2	
2 tsp.	baking powder	10	mL
1/2 tsp.	baking soda	2	mL
1 tsp.	ground cinnamon	5	mL
1 1/2 cups	whole wheat flour	375	mL
1 1/2 cups	all-purpose flour	375	mL
	Apricot or Poppy Seed Filling		

In a large bowl, cream butter, sugar, honey, vanilla, vinegar, eggs, baking powder, baking soda and cinnamon. Stir in about two-thirds of the flour. Continue adding flour until dough is firm but not dry. Chill at least 3 hours or overnight.

Preheat oven to 350°F (180°C).

On a well-floured surface, roll dough to a thickness of 1/8 inch (3 mm). Cut into 3-inch (7 cm) circles. Set circles slightly apart on lightly greased cookie sheet. Spoon a generous teaspoonful of the filling onto centre of each. Bring three edges up to form a triangle. Pinch seams together to seal. If desired, glaze by brushing with an egg yolk blended with 1 teaspoon water. Bake for 15 minutes or until edges are browned. Transfer to racks to cool. Store in airtight container for up to 3 days. If keeping longer, refrigerate or freeze. Thaw frozen cookies in refrigerator.

Makes about 2 dozen

* Use solid margarine; see page 4 for explanation.

Apricot Filling

1/2 cup	finely chopped dried apricots	125	mL
1/2 cup	finely chopped almonds or walnuts	125	mL
2 tbsp.	liquid honey	30	mL
2 tbsp.	melted butter or margarine	30	mL
1 tbsp.	fresh lemon juice	15	mL
1/4 tsp.	ground cinnamon or ginger	1	mL

In a small bowl, thoroughly combine filling ingredients.

Poppy Seed Filling

1 cup	poppy seeds	250	mL
	Boiling water		
2 tbsp.	lemon juice	30	mL
2 tbsp.	honey	30	mL
1 tbsp.	sugar	15	mL
1/4 cup	chopped walnuts (optional)	50	mL

Pour boiling water over poppy seeds and let stand overnight; drain well.
Using a food processor or blender, process the poppy seeds, lemon juice,
honey and sugar until mixture forms a paste. Stir in walnuts.

Halloween Lollipops

Guaranteed to please the little folks, and
the kids at heart — at Halloween or any time of year.
Dough requires chilling for 45 minutes.

1 cup	butter or margarine*, softened	250	mL
1 cup	granulated sugar	250	mL
1/2 cup	brown sugar	125	mL
2	eggs	2	
2 tsp.	baking powder	10	mL
1/4 tsp.	salt	1	mL
2 tsp.	vanilla	10	mL
3 cups	all-purpose flour	750	mL
30	wooden popsicle-type sticks**	30	
	Orange Icing		
	Decorations (optional)		

In a large bowl, cream butter and sugars. Beat in eggs, one at a time. Blend in vanilla, baking powder and salt. Stir in about two-thirds of the flour. Continue adding flour until dough is soft but not sticky. Chill for 45 minutes.

Preheat oven to 350°F (180°C).

Bake a test cookie; see page 6 for directions.

Pinch off 2 tablespoons (25 mL) of dough and shape into a ball. Insert wooden stick, place on lightly greased cookie sheet, and flatten dough to 1/4-inch (6 mm) thickness. Bake for 8 minutes or until nicely browned around edges. Transfer to racks to cool. Frost with Orange Icing. Decorate with candies and dried fruit, if desired.

	Orange Icing		
1/4 cup	butter or margarine, softened	50	mL
1 1/2 cups	icing sugar	375	mL
1 tbsp.	milk or undiluted orange juice concentrate	15	mL
	Red and yellow food colouring		

In a small bowl, mix together butter, icing sugar and milk until smooth. Add a few drops of red and yellow food colouring to create desired orange colour.

Makes about 30 lollipops.

* Use solid margarine; see page 4 for explanation.
** If you don't find these in a supermarket, try a hobby shop.

Variation:

Halloween Happy Faces: Shape dough into 1-inch (2.5 cm) balls. Place on greased cookie sheet about 3 inches (7 cm) apart. Using a large glass dipped in flour, flatten to 1/8-inch (3 mm) thickness. Bake, cool and frost as described. Arrange chocolate chips or candies for eyes. Using the handle of a spoon, or other suitable object, draw a smile in the icing, pressing hard enough so the icing is all removed and the cookie shows through.

Gingerbread Cookies

If you like crisp and spicy gingerbread cookies, these are the best! They can be used to make gingerbread men for Christmas, jack-o-lanterns for Halloween, or pumpkins for Thanksgiving. Dough requires chilling for 2 hours.

2/3 cup	butter or margarine*, softened	150	mL
1/2 cup	granulated sugar	125	mL
2 tsp.	ground ginger	10	mL
1 tsp.	ground cinnamon	5	mL
1/2 tsp.	ground nutmeg	2	mL
1	egg	1	
3/4 cup	molasses	175	mL
1/2 tsp.	baking powder	2	mL
1 tsp	baking soda	5	mL
3 cups	all-purpose flour	750	mL
	Raisins (optional)		
	Decorating Icing		

In a large bowl, cream butter, sugar and spices. Beat in egg, molasses, baking powder and baking soda. Blend in about two-thirds of the flour. Continue adding flour until rolling consistency is reached. Chill for 2 hours.

Preheat oven to 375°F (190°C).

On a floured surface, roll dough to 1/8-inch (3 mm) thickness (slightly thicker for tree decorations). Cut into desired shapes. Place on greased cookie sheet. For tree decorations, make a hole in the top of each with a plastic drinking straw. If desired, decorate cookies with raisins before baking, pressing them firmly into position. Bake for 8 minutes or until firm. Transfer to racks to cool. Decorate with icing piped through tube.

	Decorating Icing		
2 tbsp.	butter or margarine, softened	25	mL
2/3 cup	icing sugar	150	mL
1 tbsp.	milk	15	mL

In a small bowl, blend ingredients until smooth.
Makes 2 - 4 dozen.

* Use solid margarine; see page 4 for explanation.

Cookie Patterns

Sweet Marie Bars

Tastes like a chocolate bar!

1 tbsp.	butter	15	mL
1/2 cup	brown sugar	125	mL
1/2 cup	corn syrup	125	mL
1/2 cup	peanut butter	125	mL
2 cups	crispy rice cereal	500	mL
1/2 cup	unsalted roasted peanuts	125	mL
1 cup	chocolate chips, melted	250	mL

In a heavy saucepan over medium heat, combine butter, sugar, corn syrup and peanut butter. Stir constantly until sugar dissolves and mixture comes to a boil.

In a medium bowl, combine cereal and peanuts. Pour hot mixture over cereal and nuts; mix well. With moistened hands, press into greased 8-inch (20 cm) square pan. Spread melted chocolate on top. Cool until chocolate is just firm, about 2 hours at room temperature, before cutting into bars.

Makes about 2 dozen.

Halloween Hermits

Use leftover pumpkin for these soft, spicy cookies.
They are even good enough to warrant *opening* a can of pumpkin!

3/4 cup	shortening, softened	175	mL
1 1/4 cups	brown sugar	300	mL
2	eggs	2	
1 tsp.	vanilla	5	mL
1 cup	cooked mashed pumpkin	250	mL
2 cups	all-purpose or whole wheat flour	500	mL
1 tsp.	baking powder	5	mL
1/2 tsp.	baking soda	2	mL
1/2 tsp.	salt	2	mL
1/2 tsp.	ground cinnamon	2	mL
1/2 tsp.	ground nutmeg	2	mL
1/2 tsp.	ground allspice	2	mL
1/2 tsp.	ground cloves	2	mL
1 cup	raisins	250	mL
1 cup	chopped dates	250	mL
1/2 cup	chopped nuts	125	mL

Preheat oven to 375°F (190°C).

In a large bowl, cream shortening and sugar. Beat in eggs and vanilla, then pumpkin. Stir in flour, baking powder, baking soda, salt and spices. Mix in raisins, dates and nuts.

Bake a test cookie; see page 6 for directions.

Drop batter from a teaspoon onto greased cookie sheet. Bake for 10 minutes or until firm. Transfer to racks to cool.

Makes 4 - 5 dozen.

If you drink diet pop when eating a cookie, the calories cancel each other out.

Chocolate Valentine Hearts

The perfect Valentine treat — heart shaped,
frosted chocolate cookies.

1 cup	butter, softened	250	mL
1/3 cup	cocoa	75	mL
1 cup	icing sugar	250	mL
1 1/2 cups	all-purpose flour	375	mL
	Sweetheart Frosting		

Preheat oven to 350°F (180°C).

In a medium bowl, cream butter. Blend in cocoa and icing sugar, then flour. If dough is too soft to handle, chill for 15 minutes.

On a lightly floured surface, roll dough one-quarter at a time to a thickness of 1/8 inch (3 mm). Using cookie cutter or a paper pattern, cut dough into heart shapes. Place on greased cookie sheet. Bake for 15 minutes or until cookies seem firm. Transfer to racks to cool. Decorate cooled cookies with frosting.

Sweetheart Frosting

3 tbsp.	butter or margarine, softened	50	mL
1 cup	icing sugar	250	mL
1 tbsp.	frozen cranberry, raspberry or strawberry concentrate, thawed	15	mL

In a small bowl, blend butter, icing sugar and juice concentrate until smooth.

Makes about 3 dozen.

Children's Cottage — love in action

The Cottage nurtures children in stress. A six-year-old boy reassured his younger brother: "It's okay. Don't worry. These people are kind."

Love Knots

An attractive and tasty "special occasion" cookie — looks nice on any plate of cookies. Dough is easy to handle.

1 cup	butter or margarine*, softened	250	mL
1 cup	granulated sugar	250	mL
2	eggs	2	
1/2 cup	sour cream	125	mL
1/2 tsp	lemon flavouring	2	mL
1 tsp.	baking soda	5	mL
4 cups	all-purpose flour	1	L
	Candied cherries		

Preheat oven to 350°F (180°C).

In a large bowl, cream butter and sugar. Beat in eggs, sour cream, lemon flavouring and baking soda. Stir in about three-quarters of the flour. Continue adding flour until rolling consistency is achieved.

Bake a test cookie; see page 6 for directions.

To form knots, use a rounded teaspoonful of dough. Roll gently in hands and then on counter until piece is approximately 6 inches (15 cm) long and the diameter of a pencil. Tie in a knot and put a cherry in the centre. Place on ungreased cookie sheet. Bake for 12 minutes or until delicately browned. Transfer to racks to cool.

Makes 4 - 5 dozen.

* Use solid margarine; see page 4 for explanation.

Storing Cookies

Cookies are best stored in an airtight container. This keeps soft cookies from losing moisture and drying out. Oddly enough, it also keeps crisp cookies crisp by preventing them from absorbing moisture from the air.

San Francisco Fudge Foggies

Beyond brownies, not quite fudge — this delicious square was a contest winner from Chocolatier magazine.

1 lb.	bittersweet chocolate, finely chopped	500 g
1 cup	butter, cut into 16 pieces	250 mL
1/3 cup	strong coffee	75 mL
4	large eggs, at room temperature	4
1 1/2 cups	granulated sugar	375 mL
1/2 cup	all-purpose flour	125 mL
2 cups	coarsely-chopped walnuts	500 mL

Position a rack in the centre of the oven. Preheat oven to 375°F (190°C).

Line a 9 x 13-inch (22 x 34 cm) baking pan with a double thickness of aluminum foil, extending the foil 2 inches (5 cm) beyond sides of pan. Butter bottom and sides of foil-lined pan.

In the top of a double boiler* set over water that is hot but not simmering, combine chocolate, butter and coffee. Stir frequently until chocolate is melted and mixture is smooth. Remove from heat and cool for 10 minutes, stirring occasionally.

In a large bowl, beat eggs at high speed for 30 seconds or until foamy. Gradually add sugar. Continue to beat for 2 minutes or until very light and fluffy. Reduce speed to low and beat in chocolate mixture until just blended. Stir in flour, then walnuts, just until blended.

Spread batter in prepared pan. Bake for 20 minutes or until just set around edges and still moist in centre. Set pan on rack to cool for 30 minutes. Cover tightly with foil and refrigerate for at least 6 hours or overnight.

To serve, remove top piece of foil and run sharp knife around edge of pan. Using ends of the foil as handles, lift foggies from pan. Invert onto smooth surface. Peel off foil and cut into squares. Store in refrigerator; serve cold.

Makes about 3 dozen.

* This can also be done in a microwave oven or bowl set over hot water.

Raspberry Rings

When cut into heart shapes, this makes a wonderful Valentine
cookie. Without the jam, it's a very nice sugar cookie.
Dough requires chilling for at least 3 hours.

1 cup	butter or margarine*, softened	250 mL
1/2 cup	brown sugar	125 mL
1/2 cup	granulated sugar	125 mL
1	egg	1
1/2 tsp.	vanilla	2 mL
1 tsp.	baking soda	5 mL
1 tsp.	cream of tartar	5 mL
2 cups	all-purpose flour	500 mL
	Icing sugar	
	Raspberry jam**	

In a large bowl, cream butter. Add sugars; beat until light and fluffy.
Beat in egg, vanilla, baking soda and cream of tartar. Stir in about three-
quarters of the flour. Continue adding flour gradually until rolling consistency has been achieved. Divide dough in half, wrap in wax paper;
chill for at least 3 hours or overnight.

Preheat oven to 375°F (190°C).

Working with one portion at a time on a floured surface, using floured
rolling pin, roll dough to a thickness of 1/4 inch (6 mm) or less. Cut out
cookies. With a smaller cutter, cut a hole in the centre of half of the cookies. Place on ungreased cookie sheets, spaced about 1 1/2 inches (4 cm)
apart. Bake for 8 minutes or until lightly browned. Transfer to racks to
cool. Sprinkle icing sugar on cookies with holes. Spread whole cookies
with jam and top with sugared cookies.

Makes 2 - 4 dozen.

* Use solid margarine; see page 4 for explanation.
** Do not use freezer jam as it may mould when stored at room temperature.

Cooling Cookies

*Cool cookies on a rack, without overlapping, before placing in
storage containers.*

Sugar Fudge Cookies

Attractive and delicious.
Dough requires chilling for at least 3 hours.

1/2 cup	shortening, softened	125	mL
1 2/3 cups	granulated sugar	400	mL
2 tsp.	vanilla	10	mL
2	eggs	2	
2	squares unsweetened chocolate, melted	2	
2 tsp.	baking powder	10	mL
1/2 tsp.	salt	2	mL
2 cups	all-purpose flour	500	mL
1/3 cup	milk	75	mL
	Icing sugar		

In a large bowl, cream shortening, sugar and vanilla. Beat in eggs. Add melted chocolate, baking powder and salt; beat again. Mix in flour alternately with milk. Chill at least 3 hours.

Preheat oven to 350°F (180°C).

Bake a test cookie; see page 6 for directions.

Form into 1-inch (2.5 cm) balls; roll in icing sugar. Place on greased cookie sheet, 2 - 3 inches (5 - 7 cm) apart. Bake for 13 minutes, or until tops are cracked. Transfer to racks to cool.

Makes about 4 dozen.

Melting Chocolate Chips or Squares

Gentle heat is the key; if heat is too high, chocolate will become dry and crumbly.

Place chocolate in a small dish set in barely simmering water or in the top of a double boiler. Stir constantly to distribute heat as chocolate is melting. When about two-thirds of the chocolate is melted, remove from heat and continue stirring until completely smooth.

If using a microwave oven, use medium (50%) power and a short time. Stir at 1-minute intervals. Two squares of chocolate will take 2-3 minutes.

Receptions, Teas, Showers

Many of the celebration cookies are also suitable; see previous section.

Receptions, Teas, Showers

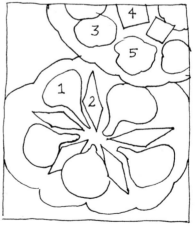

1. Calla Lilies *p. 68*
2. Caramel Pecan Bars *p. 63*
3. Daffodils *p. 66*
4. Yummy Chocolate Slice *p. 64*
5. Coconut Cherry Drops *p. 65*

Caramel Pecan Bars

Superb! To make a smaller, less expensive quantity,
halve the recipe and bake in a 9-inch (22 cm) square pan.

1 cup	butter, softened	250 mL
1/2 cup	brown sugar	125 mL
1	egg	1
3 cups	all-purpose flour	750 mL
1 1/2 cups	pecan halves	375 mL
3/4 cup	butter	175 mL
1/2 cup	liquid honey	125 mL
3/4 cup	brown sugar	175 mL
1/4 cup	whipping cream	60 mL

Preheat oven to 350°F (180°C).

In a medium bowl, cream butter and sugar. Beat in egg. Stir in flour. Press evenly in 10 x 15-inch (25 x 40 cm) jelly roll pan. Bake for 10 minutes. Remove from oven. Spread pecans evenly over crust, placing them broken side down. With a bit of planning, they can be arranged so there is a pecan in each bar when it is cut.

In a large heavy saucepan over medium heat, melt butter. Stir in honey and brown sugar. Cook, stirring constantly, until sugar dissolves and mixture boils. Continue boiling and stirring for 5 minutes or until mixture is a rich caramel colour. Remove from heat. Thoroughly blend in cream. Pour over pecans. Bake 15 minutes.

Makes 5 - 6 dozen.

Variation:

This can be turned into something akin to a pecan pie by doubling the nuts to 3 cups (750 mL).

Don't have a 10 x 15-inch jelly roll pan?

If you substitute your 9 x 13-inch pan, the bar will be considerably thicker and you may not be pleased with it. Instead, use two 9-inch square pans, and the results will be very close to the original.

Yummy Chocolate Slice

Yummy *is the word for this three-level square.*

1/2 cup	butter or margarine*, softened	125	mL
1/2 cup	brown sugar	125	mL
1/2 tsp.	almond extract (optional)	2	mL
1 cup	all-purpose flour	250	mL
1 cup	brown sugar	250	mL
1/4 cup	cocoa	60	mL
2 tbsp.	all-purpose flour	30	mL
1 tsp.	baking powder	5	mL
1/2 tsp.	salt	2	mL
3/4 cup	chopped walnuts	175	mL
2	eggs, beaten	2	
1 tsp.	vanilla	5	mL
	Chocolate Frosting		

Preheat oven to 350°F (180°C).

In a medium bowl, cream butter, the 1/2 cup (125 mL) sugar and almond extract. Stir in the 1 cup (250 mL) flour. Press into ungreased 9-inch (22 cm) square baking pan.

In another bowl, combine the 1 cup (250 mL) sugar, cocoa, 2 tablespoons (25 mL) flour, baking powder and salt. Stir in walnuts. Blend in eggs and vanilla. Spread over base.

Bake for 30 minutes or until it pulls away slightly from sides. Cool. Spread with Chocolate Frosting.

Chocolate Frosting

1/4 cup	butter or margarine, softened	60	mL
2 tbsp.	cereal cream	30	mL
1 tsp.	vanilla	5	mL
1/4 cup	cocoa	60	mL
2 cups	icing sugar	500	mL

In a medium bowl, beat ingredients until light and fluffy.
Makes about 3 dozen.

* Use solid margarine; see page 4 for explanation.

Coconut Cherry Drops

Delicious, with a nice chewy texture. Pretty on a tea tray or at Christmas time. Carries well to picnics or potlucks.

1/4 cup	butter or margarine*, softened	60 mL
1/4 cup	shortening, softened	60 mL
1/2 cup	granulated sugar	125 mL
1	egg	1
1/2 tsp.	almond extract	2 mL
1/2 tsp.	baking powder	2 mL
1/2 tsp.	salt	2 mL
1 1/4 cup	all-purpose flour	300 mL
2 tbsp.	well drained, chopped maraschino cherries	30 mL
1 cup	shredded coconut	250 mL
1/2 cup	chopped pecans	125 mL
	Maraschino cherries, halved	

Preheat oven to 375°F (190°C).

In a medium bowl, cream butter, shortening and sugar. Beat in egg, almond extract, baking powder and salt. Stir in flour. Mix in chopped cherries, coconut and pecans.

Bake a test cookie; see page 6 for directions.

Drop batter from a teaspoon onto lightly greased cookie sheet. Top with cherry halves. Bake for 10 minutes or until barely brown. Transfer to racks to cool.

Makes about 3 dozen.

* Use solid margarine; see page 4 for explanation.

Meringue Kisses

A versatile recipe, loved by children, attractive on a tea plate. The kisses are crisp on the outside and soft on the inside; the daffodils are crisp all the way through.

3	egg whites	3	
1 cup	granulated sugar	250	mL
1 tsp.	vinegar	5	mL
1 tsp.	vanilla	5	mL

Preheat oven to 250°F (120°C).

In a deep medium bowl, beat egg whites until soft peaks form. Gradually add sugar, 2 tablespoons (25 mL) at a time, while beating on medium-high speed. Add vinegar and vanilla and continue beating until mixture forms peaks that stand straight up.

Drop meringues from a teaspoon onto parchment lined or lightly-greased cookie sheet. Bake for 25 minutes or until lightly browned on bottom. Transfer to racks to cool.

Makes 5 - 6 dozen.

Variations:

Pink Kisses: Add red food colouring to meringue mixture along with vinegar and vanilla, making mixture darker than desired as colour fades during baking.

Dressed-up Meringues: Place a small dollop of pink butter icing on top of each meringue and decorate with coloured sugar, sprinkles, candied cherries, etc.

Daffodils: Follow recipe above, using 4 egg whites instead of 3; leave other ingredients the same. After dropping meringue onto cookie sheet, use back of small spoon to shape each into a small "nest" with a hollow centre and built-up sides. Bake at 200°F (100°C) for 1 hour. Turn oven off and leave meringues for another hour. Store in an airtight container. Fill with Lemon Butter just before serving.

Lemon Butter

5	eggs, beaten	5
1 1/2 cups	granulated sugar	375 mL
1/2 cup	lemon juice	125 mL
2 tbsp.	grated lemon peel	25 mL
1/2 cup	butter or margarine*	125 mL

In top of a double boiler**, combine all ingredients. Cook, stirring constantly, for 15 minutes or until thick and smooth. Refrigerate. Mixture will thicken more as it cools.

Makes about 2 3/4 cups (675 mL).

* Use solid margarine; see page 4 for explanation.
** Can also be done in a heavy pot over low heat, or in a microwave oven on medium power.

Leftover Egg Yolks

Leftover egg yolks can be stored for several days in the refrigerator. Place in cold water and cover the container to prevent them from drying out. To freeze, stir yolks gently without incorporating air. To prevent lumpiness, stir in 1/4 teaspoon (1 mL) salt or 2 teaspoons (10 mL) sugar for every 1/2 cup (125 mL) egg yolk. Place in airtight container, allowing room for expansion.

Ideas for using leftover egg yolks:

- 2 yolks are equivalent to 1 whole egg in pancakes, cookies and most cakes.
- Add to scrambled eggs, French toast, quiches and omelettes.
- Use to make hollandaise sauce or a custard.

To find out which recipes in this book use egg yolks, refer to the cross-index.

Calla Lilies

A tasty, pretty addition to a tea plate.

1	egg	1
1/4 cup	granulated sugar	50 mL
4 drops	lemon extract	4 drops
	(or a little lemon peel)	
1/3 cup	all-purpose flour	75 mL
1/4 tsp.	baking powder	1 mL
	Lemon or orange marmalade	
	or tart jelly	

Preheat oven to 325°F (160°C).

In a small bowl, beat egg until very light. Add sugar gradually, beating until thick. Beat in lemon extract. Fold in flour and baking powder.

Bake a test cookie, see page 6 for directions.

Drop batter from a teaspoon, 3 inches (7 cm) apart, onto greased cookie sheet. Bake only 4 cookies at a time. Bake for 5 minutes or until just barely golden.

Loosen immediately with a spatula and, while hot, pinch or roll one end to create a lily shape. Refer to photograph at the beginning of this section to see the shape of finished cookies. If cookies become too crisp to roll, return them briefly to the oven to soften. Place on rack to cool. Fill each lily with a dab of marmalade or jelly at serving time.

Makes about 1 dozen.

Coconut Confections

This is a versatile, colourful recipe — particularly
attractive on a mixed cookie plate.

1	can (300 mL) sweetened condensed milk	1
1 cup	icing sugar	250 mL
3 cups	medium unsweetened coconut	750 mL

In a large bowl, combine milk and icing sugar. Gradually stir in coconut until mixture is thick and barely sticky. Proceed in one of the following ways.

Ribbon Cookies: Divide dough in thirds. Add colouring and flavouring to two of the portions, leaving third portion white. Press one of the coloured portions onto a piece of wax paper to form a rectangle 6 x 9 inches (15 x 22 cm). Spread white mixture on top; press to make a smooth surface. Repeat with remaining coloured portion. Cut in half crosswise; wrap each piece tightly in foil or plastic wrap. Chill for several hours. To serve, cut crosswise in 1/2-inch (1 cm) slices, then cut into serving-size pieces.

Pinwheels: Divide dough in two; add colouring and flavouring to one portion. Press onto wax paper to form a rectangle 9 x 12 inches (22 x 30 cm). Spread white portion on top; press to make a smooth surface. Starting with the long side, roll up tightly like a jelly roll, using the wax paper to help in the rolling. Cut in two and wrap each piece tightly in foil or plastic wrap. Chill for several hours. Slice into pieces of desired size to serve.

Coconut Fruits: Divide dough into thirds, to make apricots, strawberries and limes. Into each portion, thoroughly mix 2 tablespoons (25 mL) of the appropriate jelly powder. Pinch off about 1 tablespoon (15 mL) of the mixture, and mould it into the desired fruit shape. Roll in additional jelly powder. For stems, use cloves for apricots and limes, and green icing or candied cherry for strawberries.

*When eating cookies with someone else, calories
don't count if you both eat the same amount.*

Chocolate Cherries

This recipe will please the folks who are fans of
maraschino cherry chocolates.
Dough requires chilling for 1 hour.

1/2 cup	butter or margarine*, softened	125	mL
1 1/4 cups	brown sugar	300	mL
2	eggs	2	
1 tsp.	vanilla	5	mL
1/4 cup	cocoa	60	mL
1/2 tsp.	baking soda	2	mL
1/4 tsp.	salt	1	mL
1 1/2 cups	all-purpose flour	375	mL
	Whole maraschino cherries, well drained		
	Chocolate Icing		

In a medium bowl, cream butter and sugar until fluffy. Add eggs, one at a time, beating well after each addition. Beat in vanilla. Add, in order, the cocoa, baking soda, salt and about three-quarters of the flour, stirring well after each addition. Continue adding flour to make a fairly stiff dough. Chill for 1 hour.

Preheat oven to 350°F (180°C).

Bake a test cookie; it should spread a little, but maintain some height. See page 6 for directions.

Pinch off dough in 2-teaspoon (10 mL) portions and mound on greased cookie sheet. Press a cherry lightly into top of each cookie. Bake for 10 minutes or until slightly darkened on bottom. Transfer to racks. When cool, cover each cherry with a generous dollop of Chocolate Icing. If freezing or storing a few days before using, store without icing and frost before serving.

Chocolate Icing

1 cup	icing sugar	250	mL
3 tbsp.	cocoa	50	mL
3 tbsp.	butter or margarine, softened	50	mL
	Boiling water		

In a small bowl, combine ingredients using enough boiling water to make a soft icing.

Makes 4 - 5 dozen.

* Use solid margarine; see page 4 for explanation.

Variation:

Omit cherries and add 1/2 cup (125 mL) chopped walnuts or pecans to batter. Bake as directed.

Cookies make a wonderful gift!

Empire Biscuits

A little more work to make, but worth the effort.
Dough requires chilling for 1 hour.

1/2 cup	butter or margarine*, softened	125 mL
1/4 tsp.	ground mace	1 mL
1/4 tsp.	ground cinnamon	1 mL
1/4 cup	granulated sugar	50 mL
1 1/4 cups	all-purpose flour	300 mL
	Currant jelly	
	Glaze	
	Candied red and green cherries, cut in pieces	

In a medium bowl, cream butter and spices. Beat in sugar. Gradually stir in flour to make a soft dough. Chill for 1 hour or until dough is stiff enough to handle.

Preheat oven to 400°F (200°C).

On a lightly-floured surface, roll to 1/16-inch (2 mm) thickness. Cut with a 1 1/2-inch (4 cm) round cookie cutter. Place on ungreased cookie sheet. Bake 4 minutes or until lightly browned around the edges. Transfer to racks to cool. Sandwich two cookies together with a thin layer of currant jelly. Spread glaze over tops of sandwiched cookies. Garnish with bits of red and green cherries.

Glaze

1 cup	sifted icing sugar	250 mL
4 tsp.	water	20 mL

In a small bowl, thoroughly combine icing sugar and water.

Makes about 2 dozen.

* Use solid margarine; see page 4 for explanation.

Spritz Cookies

Tastes great; dough is easy to work with.

1 cup	butter, softened	250 mL
1/2 cup	granulated sugar	125 mL
1	egg	1
1 tsp.	vanilla	5 mL
1/2 tsp.	salt	2 mL
2 1/2 cups	all-purpose flour	625 mL

Preheat oven to 350°F (180°C).

In a medium bowl, cream butter and sugar. Beat in egg, vanilla and salt. Stir in about three-quarters of the flour. Continue adding flour slowly until dough is right consistency for putting through a cookie press.

Put dough through press onto ungreased cookie sheet, shaping as desired. Bake for 15 minutes or until golden on the bottom.

Makes 4 - 5 dozen.

Overnight Cookies

These heavenly cookies, sometimes called "Sleepers",
are a nice variation of the traditional macaroon-type of cookie.

2	egg whites	2
1 tsp.	vanilla	5 mL
1/8 tsp.	salt	0.5 mL
2/3 cup	berry sugar	150 mL
1 cup	chocolate chips	250 mL
1 cup	coarsely chopped walnuts or pecans	250 mL

Preheat oven to 350°F (180°C).

In a deep small bowl, beat egg whites with vanilla and salt until foamy. Gradually beat in sugar, 2 tablespoons (25 mL) at a time, until stiff peaks form and no granules of sugar can be felt when a bit of the meringue is rubbed between finger and thumb. Stir in chocolate chips and nuts.

Drop meringue from a teaspoon onto cookie sheet covered with aluminum foil, brown paper or cooking parchment. Garnish with additional chocolate chips, if desired. Place in oven and turn off heat. Do not open oven door for at least 6 hours or overnight.

Makes about 4 dozen.

Leftover Egg Whites

Leftover egg whites may be refrigerated for several days in a tightly-covered container. For longer storage, freeze in an airtight container, allowing room for expansion.

Leftover egg whites can be used in meringues, macaroons, souffles, scrambled eggs and omelettes, and to glaze crusts of bread and pastries before baking. You can also dip cookie garnishes into unbeaten egg white before pressing them onto the cookie. This gives them a nice sheen. Some people use egg whites as a facial mask.

Refer to the cross-index to find which recipes in the book use egg whites.

Mexican Mocha Balls

An interesting and tasty "shortbread" type of cookie.
Dough requires chilling for 1 hour.

1 cup	butter or margarine*, softened	250	mL
1/2 cup	granulated sugar	125	mL
1 tsp.	vanilla	5	mL
1/4 cup	cocoa	60	mL
1 tsp.	instant coffee crystals	5	mL
1/4 tsp.	salt	1	mL
2 cups	all-purpose flour	500	mL
1/2 cup	well-drained, finely chopped maraschino cherries	125	mL
1/2 cup	finely chopped walnuts or pecans	125	mL
	Granulated sugar		

In a medium bowl, cream butter, sugar and vanilla. Beat in cocoa, coffee crystals and salt. Stir in flour, then cherries and nuts. Chill 1 hour.

Preheat oven to 325°F (160°C).

Bake a test cookie; see page 6 for directions.

Form dough into 1-inch (2.5 cm) balls. Shake a few at a time in a bag with granulated sugar. Place on ungreased cookie sheet and bake for 20 minutes or until top starts to crack. Transfer to racks to cool. If desired, drizzle a little melted chocolate over cooled Mocha Balls.

Makes 3 - 4 dozen.

* Use solid margarine; see page 4 for explanation.

Lemon Caraway Cookies

A unique surprise and a favourite with caraway lovers.
Dough requires chilling for 6 hours.

3/4 cup	butter or margarine*, softened	175 mL
1 cup	granulated sugar	250 mL
1	egg	1
1 tbsp.	lemon juice	15 mL
2 cups	all-purpose flour	500 mL
1 tsp.	caraway seeds	5 mL
1 tsp.	grated lemon peel	5 mL
2 cups	corn flake cereal, finely crushed	500 mL
1/4 tsp.	baking soda	1 mL
1/2 tsp.	salt	2 mL

In a medium bowl, cream butter and sugar. Beat in egg and lemon juice. Stir in about three-quarters of the flour, along with remaining ingredients. Continue adding flour until dough is soft but not sticky. Shape into rolls about 2 inches (5 cm) in diameter. Wrap in plastic or wax paper. Chill 6 hours or until firm.

Preheat oven to 375°F (190°C).

With a thin sharp knife, cut roll into 1/4-inch (6 mm) slices. Place on ungreased cookie sheet. Bake for 8 minutes or until pale gold. Transfer to racks to cool.

Makes about 4 dozen.

* Use solid margarine; see page 4 for explanation.

Shaping Refrigerator Cookies

Modern recipes for refrigerator cookies direct us to roll the dough into logs, wrap them and refrigerate until ready to slice. In the late '20s, there was a different approach. Recipes advised the cook to press the dough into a loaf pan, chill it, then slice and bake. For smaller cookies, the "loaf" of dough could be cut lengthwise before slicing.

Children's Cottage Cookie Cook Book

Date Pinwheels

Time-consuming to make, but a treat from the past.
Dough requires chilling.

1/2 cup	butter or margarine*, softened	125	mL
1 cup	brown sugar	250	mL
1	egg	1	
1 3/4 cup	all-purpose flour	425	mL
1 tsp.	baking powder	5	mL
1/4 tsp.	salt	1	mL
1/4 tsp.	cinnamon	1	mL
1/4 tsp.	cloves	1	mL
	Date Filling		

In a medium bowl, cream butter. Gradually add sugar and continue beating. Add egg, beating thoroughly. Stir in 1 cup (250 mL) of the flour, along with the baking powder, salt and spices. Gradually mix in remaining flour until dough is of rolling consistency. Chill for 1 hour.

Prepare date filling while dough is chilling.

Divide dough in half. On unfloured wax paper, roll one portion of dough into a rectangle 6 x 12 inches (15 x 30 cm). Spread with half of date mixture. Starting with long side, roll up snugly like a jelly roll. Repeat with remaining dough. Chill again for 1 hour.

Preheat oven to 375°F (190°C).

Using a thin sharp knife, cut cookie roll into 1/4-inch (6 mm) slices. Place on greased cookie sheet. Bake for 12 minutes or until golden brown on bottom. Transfer to racks to cool.

	Date Filling		
1 1/2 cups	chopped dates	375	mL
1/2 cup	water	125	mL
1 tsp.	lemon juice	5	mL
1/2 cup	finely-chopped peanuts (optional)	125	mL

In a heavy saucepan over low heat, cook dates, water and lemon juice until thick. Stir often and add a little more water if necessary. Cool. Add peanuts. Makes 5 - 6 dozen.

* Use solid margarine; see page 4 for explanation.

Unbaked Butterscotch Squares

A popular choice for both family and special occasions.

1	package (300 g) butterscotch chips	1	
1/4 cup	butter or margarine*	50	mL
3/4 cup	peanut butter	175	mL
1 1/4 cups	miniature marshmallows	300	mL

In a heavy saucepan, combine butterscotch chips, butter and peanut butter. Cook and stir over medium heat until melted and combined. Cool almost to room temperature. (Mixture must be cool to prevent marshmallows from melting. If unsure, test with one marshmallow first.)

Stir in marshmallows. Spread in 8-inch (20 cm) square baking pan. Let stand at room temperature for about 2 hours, or until set.

Makes about 2 dozen.

Variation:

Add 1/2 cup (125 mL) finely chopped nuts or 1 cup cereal flakes or puffed cereal, or both.

* Use solid margarine; see page 4 for explanation.

Cherry Bars

A delicious addition to a tea tray or Christmas cookie plate.

1 1/2 cups	all-purpose flour	375 mL
1/4 cup	icing sugar	50 mL
1/2 cup	butter	125 mL
2	eggs	2
1 cup	brown sugar	250 mL
1/2 cup	coconut	125 mL
1/2 cup	chopped walnuts	125 mL
1 cup	coarsely-chopped red candied cherries	250 mL
	Lemon Butter Icing	

Preheat oven to 350°F (180°C).

In a medium bowl, combine flour and icing sugar. Rub or cut in butter until mixture resembles coarse crumbs. Press into ungreased 8-inch (20 cm) square pan. Bake for 8 minutes. Remove from oven.

In the same bowl, beat eggs. Add brown sugar and beat again. Stir in coconut, walnuts and cherries. Spread evenly over partially-baked base. Bake for 30 minutes or until golden. When cool, frost with Lemon Butter Icing.

Lemon Butter Icing

1 cup	icing sugar	250 mL
2 tbsp	butter or margarine, softened	25 mL
1 tbsp.	lemon juice	15 mL
1/4 tsp.	grated lemon rind	1 mL

In a small bowl, thoroughly combine icing sugar, butter, lemon juice and rind. Add a small amount of boiling water, if required, to achieve spreading consistency.

Makes about 2 dozen.

Lemon Pecan Bars

A delicious old favourite;
the pecans give it a contemporary twist.

1/2 cup	butter or margarine*, softened	125 mL
1/4 cup	icing sugar	50 mL
1 cup	all-purpose flour	250 mL
1/2 cup	chopped pecans (optional)	125 mL
2	eggs	2
1 cup	granulated sugar	250 mL
2 tbsp.	all-purpose flour	25 mL
1/2 tsp.	baking powder	2 mL
1/4 tsp.	salt	1 mL
3 tbsp.	lemon juice	50 mL
1 tsp.	grated lemon peel	5 mL
	Icing sugar	

Preheat oven to 350°F (180°C).

In a medium bowl, cream butter and icing sugar. Mix in the 1 cup (250 mL) flour and the pecans. Press into greased 8-inch (20 cm) square baking pan. Bake for 20 minutes.

In the same bowl, beat remaining ingredients except icing sugar for about 3 minutes or until light and fluffy. Pour over base and bake for 20 minutes or until top is golden. Cool in pan. Sprinkle with icing sugar.

Makes about 2 dozen.

* Use solid margarine; see page 4 for explanation.

From a 1905 Cookbook—Clear instructions for zesting a lemon, as we call it today:

"To Grate Lemon Peel—There is a right and wrong way to grate it. The flavour comes from an essential oil found only in the yellow rind at the surface. The white part underneath is bitter, contains no lemon flavour, will curdle milk or cream, and is objectionable. Therefore, grate a lemon carefully, aiming to remove all the yellow surface, but no more."

Cheesecake Bars

This is an excellent recipe; useful for large family or special-event gatherings.

2 cups	all-purpose or whole wheat flour	500 mL
1 1/2 cups	brown sugar	375 mL
1 cup	butter or margarine*	250 mL
1 1/2 cups	rolled oats	375 mL
2	packages (250 g each) cream cheese, softened	2
1/2 cup	granulated sugar	125 mL
3	eggs	3
1/4 cup	milk	50 mL
1 tsp.	vanilla	5 mL
1/4 cup	lemon juice	50 mL
	Jam, jelly or lemon spread** (optional)	

Preheat oven to 350°F (180°C).

In a medium bowl, combine flour and brown sugar. Using a pastry blender or two knives, cut in butter until mixture resembles coarse crumbs. Stir in rolled oats. Set aside 1 1/2 cups (375 mL) of mixture. Press remainder into ungreased 10 x 15-inch (25 x 40 cm) jelly roll pan. Bake for 10 minutes.

In another bowl, beat cream cheese and sugar until fluffy. Add eggs; beat well. Beat in milk, vanilla and lemon juice. Pour over crust. Sprinkle with reserved crumbs. Bake for 25 minutes or until lightly browned. Cool; store in refrigerator. Just before serving, top each bar with a dab of jam or jelly.

Makes 5 - 6 dozen.

* Use solid margarine; see page 4 for explanation.
** For Lemon Butter recipe, see page 67.

Pecan Pie Bars

This two-layered bar is sweet and gooey,
a favourite with pecan pie lovers.

1 cup	vanilla wafer crumbs	250 mL
1/2 cup	all-purpose or whole wheat flour	125 mL
1/2 tsp.	baking powder	2 mL
1 3/4 cup	brown sugar, divided	425 mL
1/2 cup	melted butter	125 mL
2	eggs	2
2 tsp.	vanilla	10 mL
1	package (100 g) pecans, coarsely chopped	1

Preheat oven to 350°F (180°C).

In a medium bowl, combine wafer crumbs, flour, baking powder and 1 cup (250 mL) of the brown sugar. Thoroughly stir in melted butter. Mixture will be crumbly. Press into greased 8-inch (20 cm) square baking pan. Bake for 10 minutes.

In the same bowl, beat eggs. Beat in remaining 3/4 cup (175 mL) sugar and the vanilla. Stir in pecans. Pour evenly over crust. Return to oven and continue baking for 20 minutes until topping is set.

Makes about 2 dozen.

To make vanilla or graham wafer crumbs

Here are two quick and easy methods.
- *Place wafers in blender or food processor; process until crumbs are of desired texture.*
- *Or place wafers in a plastic bag; crush with a rolling pin until they are as fine as desired.*

Apricot Coconut Cookie Bars

A different, delicious, delicately flavoured bar.

1 cup	all-purpose or whole wheat flour	250	mL
1/4 cup	granulated sugar	50	mL
1/2 cup	butter or margarine*	125	mL
1/2 cup	all-purpose flour	125	mL
1/2 tsp.	baking powder	2	mL
1/4 tsp.	salt	1	mL
2	eggs, beaten	2	
1	can (300 mL) sweetened condensed milk	1	
1 1/3 cup	coconut	325	mL
1 cup	chopped dried apricots	250	mL

Preheat oven to 350°F (180°C).

In a medium bowl, stir together the 1 cup (250 mL) flour and sugar. Using a pastry blender or two knives, cut in butter until mixture resembles coarse crumbs. Press firmly into ungreased 9-inch (22 cm) square baking pan. Bake for 25 minutes or until edges are lightly browned.

Reduce oven temperature to 300°F (150°C).

In the same bowl, combine the 1/2 cup (125 mL) flour, baking powder and salt. Thoroughly stir in eggs and milk. Mix in coconut and apricots. Spread on base. Bake for 30 minutes or until golden on top.

Makes about 2 dozen.

* Use solid margarine; see page 4 for explanation.

Freezing cookies and bars

Most cookies and bars freeze well when carefully packed in moisture-proof wrappings. Icing is generally better fresh, so freeze bars and cookies unfrosted, and ice once thawed.

Cherry Chews

Popular and pretty.

Base

1 cup	all-purpose flour	250	mL
1 cup	rolled oats	250	mL
1/2 cup	brown sugar	125	mL
1 tsp.	baking powder	5	mL
1/2 cup	butter or margarine*, melted	125	mL

Filling

3	eggs, slightly beaten	3	
1 1/2 cups	brown sugar	375	mL
3 tbsp.	flour	50	mL
1 1/2 tsp.	baking powder	7	mL
1/2 tsp.	salt	2	mL
1 cup	coconut	250	mL
1 cup	coarsely chopped maraschino cherries	250	mL
	Cherry Frosting		

Preheat oven to 350°F (180°C).

In a medium bowl, prepare base by combining the flour, rolled oats, brown sugar and baking powder. Thoroughly mix in melted butter. Press into 9 x 13-inch (22 x 34 cm) baking pan. Bake for 10 minutes.

In the same bowl, prepare filling by combining eggs, brown sugar, flour, baking powder and salt. Stir in coconut and cherries. Spread over base. Bake for 30 minutes or until golden. Ice with Cherry Frosting while hot.

Cherry Frosting

2 cups	icing sugar	500	mL
1/4 cup	butter or margarine, softened	50	mL
3 tbsp	maraschino cherry juice	50	mL
	Boiling water		

In a medium bowl, combine icing sugar, butter and cherry juice. Gradually stir in boiling water until icing is of spreading consistency. Makes about 3 dozen.

* Use solid margarine; see page 4 for explanation.

Orange-Caramel Bars

Our tasters rated these tops!

2	eggs	2	
1 1/2 cups	brown sugar	375	mL
1 1/3 cups	all-purpose flour	325	mL
2/3 cup	cut-up* fresh orange slices	150	mL
2/3 cup	chopped pecans	150	mL
	Orange Glaze		

Preheat oven to 350°F (180°C).

In a medium bowl, beat eggs. Add sugar and beat on high speed for 3 minutes. Stir in flour. Mix in orange pieces and pecans. Spread in greased 10 x 15-inch (25 x 40 cm) jelly roll pan. Bake for 30 minutes or until nicely browned. While warm, spread with Orange Glaze.

Orange Glaze

2/3 cup	icing sugar	150	mL
2 tbsp.	cream or milk	25	mL
	Grated rind of one orange		

In a small bowl, mix until smooth.

Makes 4 - 6 dozen.

* Cut orange slices into small pieces.

Nanaimo Bars

An old favourite — and with good reason.

1/2 cup	butter	125	mL
1/4 cup	granulated sugar	50	mL
5 tbsp.	cocoa	75	mL
1	egg, beaten	1	
1 tsp.	vanilla	5	mL
1 1/2 cups	graham wafer crumbs	375	mL
1 cup	coconut	250	mL
1/2 cup	finely chopped walnuts	125	mL
1/4 cup	butter, softened	50	mL
3 tbsp.	milk	45	mL
2 tbsp.	vanilla custard powder	30	mL
2 cups	icing sugar	500	mL
4	squares semi-sweet chocolate, melted	4	

In a heavy saucepan over medium heat, melt the 1/2 cup (125 mL) butter. Stir in granulated sugar and cocoa. Remove from heat. Mix in egg and vanilla. Stir in crumbs, then coconut and nuts. Press into ungreased 8-inch (20 cm) square pan.

In a small bowl, cream the 1/4 cup (50 mL) butter, milk, custard powder and icing sugar until well blended. Spread over base. Place in freezer to set slightly (about 7 minutes).

Spread melted chocolate over custard layer. Store in refrigerator.

Makes about 2 dozen.

Graham Wafer Crumbs

Some people have found that the base of their tried-and-true Nanaimo Bars has become too crumbly, even though they aren't doing anything different—or so they think.

Investigation usually shows that they used to make their own graham wafer crumbs and now are buying the prepackaged ones. Prepackaged crumbs are finer, so absorb more moisture. Therefore, it may be necessary to reduce the quantity by about one-quarter in some recipes.

Children's Cottage Cookie Cook Book

Raspberry Dream Bars

This bar is two-layered, colourful and yummy.

Base

1 1/3 cups	all-purpose flour	325	mL
1/3 cup	granulated sugar	75	mL
1/2 tsp.	baking powder	2	mL
1/4 tsp.	salt	1	mL
1/2 cup	butter or margarine*	125	mL
1	egg, slightly beaten	1	

Filling

2	eggs, beaten	2	
1 1/2 cups	brown sugar	375	mL
2 tbsp.	all-purpose flour	25	mL
1 tsp.	baking powder	5	mL
1/4 tsp.	salt	1	mL
1/2 tsp.	vanilla	2	mL
1/2 cup	coconut	125	mL
1/2 cup	chopped walnuts (optional)	125	mL
1/4 cup	raspberry jam**	50	mL

Preheat oven to 375°F (190°C).

In a medium bowl, prepare base by combining flour, granulated sugar, baking powder and salt. Using a pastry blender or two knives, cut in butter until mixture resembles coarse crumbs. Stir in egg. Mix thoroughly with hands. Pat evenly into 9-inch (22 cm) square baking pan. Bake for 10 minutes.

Reduce heat to 350°F (180°C).

In the same bowl, prepare filling by combining the eggs, brown sugar, flour, baking powder, salt and vanilla. Mix in coconut and nuts.

Spread jam over partially-baked base. Spoon coconut mixture on top and spread carefully. Bake 20 minutes or until firm.

Makes about 2 dozen.

* Use solid margarine; see page 4 for explanation.
** Do not use freezer jam; it has a different consistency and may not bake well.

Almond Shortbread Fingers

An easy, delicious, large-quantity shortbread.
Dough requires overnight chilling.

1	package (1 lb/454 g) unsalted butter, softened (do not use margarine)	1
1 3/4 cups	sugar	425 mL
2	eggs	2
1	package (200 g) marzipan	1
1 tsp.	almond extract	5 mL
1 cup	finely-chopped or ground almonds	250 mL
1/4 tsp.	baking soda	1 mL
1/2 tsp.	salt	2 mL
4 3/4 cups	all-purpose flour	1175 mL

In a large bowl, cream butter and sugar until the consistency of whipped cream. Add eggs and beat for a few more minutes. Beat in marzipan, almond extract, almonds, baking soda and salt. Stir in about three-quarters of the flour. Continue adding flour until dough is soft and only slightly sticky.

Line a 10 x 15 inch (25 x 40 cm) jelly roll pan with wax paper. Pat dough into pan. Cover with wax paper and press dough until even. Chill 8 hours or overnight.

Preheat oven to 350°F (180°C).

Remove top piece of wax paper from chilled dough, invert onto cutting board, and remove second piece of wax paper. Cut dough into strips about 1/2 x 2 1/2 inches (1 x 6 cm). Place on ungreased cookie sheet about 1 inch (2.5 cm) apart. Bake for 12 minutes or until pale gold. Transfer to racks to cool.

Makes about 10 dozen.

To Prevent Overbaking

When cookies are baked, remove from cookie sheets immediately unless otherwise directed.

Children's Cottage Cookie Cook Book

Family Favourites

Family Favourites

1. *Choco Chunkies p. 91*
2. *Ginger Creams p. 92*

Choco Chunkies

The home economist who tested this recipe reported: "the most favourite cookie around our house ever! It seemed to be the chunks that everyone liked!"

1 1/2 cups	smooth or crunchy peanut butter	375 mL
1/2 cup	butter or margarine*, softened	125 mL
3/4 cup	granulated sugar	175 mL
2/3 cup	brown sugar	150 mL
2	eggs	2
1 1/2 tsp.	vanilla	7 mL
1/2 tsp.	baking soda	2 mL
1 cup	rolled oats	250 mL
3/4 cup	all-purpose or whole wheat flour	175 mL
8	squares semi-sweet chocolate, each square cut into 8 pieces	8

Preheat oven to 350°F (180°C).

In a medium bowl, cream peanut butter and butter. Gradually beat in sugars. Blend in eggs, vanilla and baking soda. Mix in rolled oats and flour. Stir in chocolate chunks.

Bake a test cookie; see page 6 for directions.

Drop dough from a tablespoon onto greased cookie sheet. Fill only one sheet at a time, and refrigerate remaining dough until ready to do the next sheet. Bake for 10 minutes or until centres are still soft to touch. Let stand 3 minutes, then transfer to racks to cool completely.

Makes about 3 dozen.

* Use solid margarine; see page 4 for explanation.

Timing Cookies

Because cookies are small, they are easily overbaked. The baking time specified in a recipe is just a guideline, so our recipes also describe how to tell when the cookies are ready to be removed from the oven.

Ginger Creams

These soft, spicy cookies have a cake-like texture.

1/4 cup	shortening, softened	50 mL
1/2 cup	granulated sugar	125 mL
1/2 tsp.	salt	2 mL
1 tsp.	ground ginger	5 mL
1/2 tsp.	ground nutmeg	2 mL
1/2 tsp.	ground cloves	2 mL
1/2 tsp.	ground cinnamon	2 mL
1	egg	1
1/2 cup	molasses	125 mL
1/2 cup	boiling water	125 mL
1 tsp.	baking soda	5 mL
2 cups	all-purpose flour	500 mL
	Vanilla Butter Icing	

In a medium bowl, cream shortening, sugar, salt and spices. Beat in egg, then molasses.

In a measuring cup, combine boiling water and baking soda. Stir into creamed mixture. Blend in flour. Mixture will have consistency of cake batter. Chill 1 hour.

Preheat oven to 350°F (180°C).

Bake a test cookie; see page 6 for directions.

Drop batter from a teaspoon onto greased cookie sheet. Bake for 7 minutes or until top springs back when lightly touched in centre. Transfer to racks to cool. Ice with Vanilla Butter Icing.

Vanilla Butter Icing

3 tbsp.	butter or margarine, softened	50 mL
3/4 cup	icing sugar	175 mL
1 tsp.	vanilla	5 mL

In a small bowl, combine ingredients until smooth. If necessary, add a few drops of water or milk to achieve spreading consistency.

Makes about 3 dozen.

Easy Date-Filled Oatmeal Cookies

An easy drop version of an old-time favourite.

1 cup	butter	250	mL
1 cup	brown sugar	250	mL
1	egg	1	
2 tsp.	vanilla	10	mL
1/2 tsp	baking soda	2	mL
1/2 tsp.	salt	2	mL
1/2 tsp.	cinnamon	2	mL
1 1/2 cups	all-purpose or whole wheat flour	375	mL
1 1/2 cups	rolled oats	375	mL
	Date Filling		

Preheat oven to 350°F (180°C).

In a large bowl, cream butter and sugar. Beat in egg, vanilla, baking soda, salt and cinnamon. Blend in flour. Stir in rolled oats.

Bake a test cookie; see page 6 for directions.

For each cookie, use about half a tablespoon (7 mL). Drop onto greased cookie sheet, leaving about 2 inches (5 cm) between cookies. With bottom of a glass dipped in flour, flatten each cookie to a thickness of a little less than 1/4 inch (5 mm). Bake for 7 minutes or until golden brown. Cool on cookie sheet for about 2 minutes, then transfer to racks to cool completely. Spread date filling on one cooled cookie and top with a second.

Date Filling

1 cup	chopped dates	250	mL
1/2 cup	water	125	mL
	Granulated sugar (optional)		

In a heavy saucepan, combine dates and water. Bring to a boil, then reduce heat to low. Cook until smooth and thick, stirring often. Add a little more water if needed. Add a little sugar if desired.

Makes about 2 dozen filled cookies.

Refrigerator Cookies

The following quote from a 1938 cookbook gives us an insight as to the origin of "ice box" cookies. "Cookie making is not the tedious task that it used to be. The old-time cook rolled her dough, cut the cookies, then rolled the scraps again, all of which took up much time. The modern housewife frequently makes her cookies without benefit of rolling pin, by slicing off portions as the cookies are required."

1 cup	butter or margarine*, softened	250 mL
1 1/2 cups	brown sugar	375 mL
2	eggs	2
1 tsp.	vanilla	5 mL
1 tsp.	baking soda	5 mL
1/4 tsp.	salt	1 mL
3 cups	all-purpose flour	750 mL

In a large bowl, cream butter and sugar until fluffy. Beat in eggs, vanilla, baking soda and salt. Stir in about two-thirds of the flour. Continue to mix in flour until dough is soft but not sticky.

On a floured surface, shape dough into two smooth rolls about 1 1/2 inches (4 cm) in diameter. Wrap in wax paper and chill at least 8 hours or up to 1 week. For longer storage, wrap unbaked rolls in plastic and freeze.

Preheat oven to 375°F (190°C).

Using a thin sharp knife, cut into 1/8-inch (3 mm) slices. Place on ungreased cookie sheet. Bake for 8 minutes or until lightly browned. Transfer to racks to cool.

Makes about 11 dozen.

* Use solid margarine; see page 4 for explanation.

Variations:

Cookie Tarts: Follow basic recipe. When cookies are sliced, spoon 1 teaspoon (5 mL) red jam or jelly on half the slices. Top with rest of slices. Seal edges. Cut slits in top so filling shows through.

Butterscotch Nut: Follow basic recipe. Mix 1/2 cup (125 mL) chopped nuts into dough.

Chocolate Nut: Follow basic recipe. Blend 3 squares (3 oz.) unsweetened chocolate, melted and cooled, into the butter mixture. Mix 1/2 cup (125 mL) chopped nuts into dough.

Fruit: Follow basic recipe. Mix in 2/3 cup (150 mL) chopped candied fruit or maraschino cherries.

Ginger: Follow basic recipe except blend 1/4 cup molasses into the butter mixture, omitting the vanilla. Add 1 1/2 tsp. (7 mL) ginger and 1 tsp. (5 mL) cinnamon to flour. Add extra flour if needed.

Orange: Follow basic recipe except add 1 tbsp. (15 mL) grated orange peel, 1 tsp. (5 mL) grated lemon peel and 1 tbsp. (15 mL) orange juice to the butter mixture, omitting the vanilla. Granulated sugar may be substituted for part or all of the brown sugar.

Pistachio: Follow basic recipe except substitute 1/2 tsp. (2 mL) almond extract and 1/2 tsp. (2 mL) grated orange peel for the vanilla. Mix 1/2 cup (125 mL) chopped pistachios into dough.

Lemon Almond: Follow basic recipe except substitute 3 tablespoons (50 mL) lemon juice and 3 tablespoons (50 mL) grated lemon peel for the vanilla. Granulated sugar may be substituted for part or all of the brown sugar. Stir 1 cup (250 mL) slivered almonds into dough. If necessary, add 1/4 - 1/2 cup (50 - 125 mL) extra flour.

OR follow the advice given in the same 1938 cookbook quoted earlier. *"To make a variety of cookies, and at the same time lessen the work, double or treble a basic recipe. Divide the dough into four portions. Bake one lot plain; mix some nuts with another portion; flavour the third portion with chocolate; and in the fourth use raisins, peel, coconut, cherries or other fruit. If desired, frost the plain cookies with chocolate frosting, and the chocolate cookies with plain frosting."*

Refrigerator cookies are practical, especially for small families, because you can bake only as many as you need at a particular time.

Snickerdoodles

Slightly crisp — everybody's favourite. Kids love the name!

1/2 cup	shortening, softened	125	mL
1/2 cup	butter or margarine*, softened	125	mL
1 1/2 cups	granulated sugar	375	mL
1/4 tsp.	salt	1	mL
1 tsp.	cream of tartar	5	mL
1 tsp.	baking soda	5	mL
1 tsp.	vanilla	5	mL
2	eggs	2	
2 1/2 cups	all-purpose or whole wheat flour	625	mL
2 tbsp.	granulated sugar	25	mL
1 tsp.	ground cinnamon	5	mL

Preheat oven to 375°F (190°C).

In a large bowl, cream shortening, butter, the 1 1/2 cups (375 mL) sugar, salt, cream of tartar, baking soda and vanilla. Beat in eggs. Stir in flour.

Bake a test cookie; see page 6 for directions.

Shape dough into balls the size of walnuts. Shake the balls, a few at a time, in a bag with the 2 tablespoons (25 mL) sugar and the cinnamon. Place about 3 inches (7 cm) apart on ungreased cookie sheet. Bake for 12 minutes or until lightly browned but still soft. Transfer to racks to cool.

Makes 3 - 4 dozen.

* Use solid margarine; see page 4 for explanation.

Freeze cookie dough for almost-instant cookies.

Mix up cookie dough, bake part, and freeze the rest in batches. Bake as required. This way you always have fresh-baked cookies readily available.

Applesauce Oatmeal Cookies

A spicy, moist family favourite.

1/2 cup	shortening, softened	125	mL
3/4 cup	granulated sugar	175	mL
1	egg	1	
1/2 tsp.	salt	2	mL
1 tsp.	ground cinnamon	5	mL
1/2 tsp.	ground nutmeg	2	mL
1/2 tsp.	ground cloves	2	mL
1 cup	sweetened applesauce	250	mL
1 tsp.	baking soda	5	mL
1 3/4 cups	all-purpose or whole wheat flour	425	mL
1 cup	raisins	250	mL
1 cup	rolled oats	250	mL

Preheat oven to 350°F (180°C).

In a large bowl, cream shortening and sugar. Beat in egg, salt and spices.

In a small bowl, combine applesauce and baking soda. Blend into creamed mixture alternately with flour. Stir in raisins and rolled oats.

Bake a test cookie; see page 6 for directions.

Drop batter from a teaspoon onto greased cookie sheet. Bake for 15 minutes or until golden brown. Transfer to racks to cool.

Makes about 3 dozen.

Banana Drop Cookies

Easy and good-tasting — great way to use that ripe banana.

3/4 cup	shortening, softened	175	mL
1 cup	granulated sugar	250	mL
1	egg	1	
1 cup	mashed ripe banana	250	mL
1/2 tsp.	baking soda	2	mL
1/2 tsp.	salt	2	mL
1 tsp.	ground cinnamon	5	mL
1/4 tsp.	ground nutmeg	1	mL
1 1/2 cups	all-purpose or whole wheat flour	375	mL
1 3/4 cups	rolled oats	425	mL
1 cup	nuts or chocolate chips (optional)	250	mL

Preheat oven to 375°F (190°C).

In a large bowl, cream shortening and sugar. Beat in egg, banana, baking soda, salt and spices. Stir in flour. Mix in rolled oats and nuts or chocolate chips.

Bake a test cookie; see page 6 for directions.

Drop batter from a teaspoon onto ungreased cookie sheet. Bake for 12 minutes or until nicely browned. Transfer to racks to cool.

Makes about 4 dozen.

Many cookie doughs and batters for bars can easily be blended together with a wooden spoon or rubber spatula, or you can use an electric beater if you find it more convenient.

Sour Cream Sugar Cookies

Favourite at Christmas or any other time of the year.
Dough requires overnight chilling.

1 cup	shortening, softened	250	mL
1 1/2 cups	granulated sugar	375	mL
3/4 cup	sour cream	175	mL
2	eggs	2	
1 tsp.	vanilla	5	mL
2 tsp.	baking powder	10	mL
1 tsp.	baking soda	5	mL
3 1/2 cups	all-purpose flour	875	mL
	Granulated sugar		

In a large bowl, cream shortening and sugar. Beat in sour cream, then eggs, vanilla, baking powder and baking soda. Stir in about three-quarters of the flour. Continue adding flour gradually until dough is soft but not sticky. Cover and chill overnight.

Preheat oven to 350°F (180°C).

On a lightly-floured surface, roll dough to 3/8-inch (9 mm) thickness. Cut into desired shapes. Place on ungreased cookie sheet. Sprinkle with sugar. Bake for 12 minutes or until just slightly browned. Transfer to racks to cool.

Makes 5 - 6 dozen.

Variation:

For Christmas, these can be sprinkled with red or green sugar. For a crisp cookie, roll thinner and reduce baking time.

Chewy Coconut Macaroons

Chewy, easy to make — an old favourite.

3 cups	sweetened flaked coconut	750 mL
1/2 cup	all-purpose flour	125 mL
1/4 tsp.	salt	1 mL
1	can (300 mL) sweetened condensed milk	1
1 tsp	vanilla	5 mL
	Candied cherries, cut in pieces (optional)	

Preheat oven to 325°F (160°C).

In a large bowl, combine coconut, flour and salt. Stir in milk and vanilla.

Drop from a tablespoon onto a greased or parchment-lined cookie sheet. Decorate each with a piece of cherry, if desired. Bake for 13 minutes or until golden brown around the edges. Cool on cookie sheet for a few minutes, then transfer to racks to cool completely.

Makes 2 dozen (large).

Variation:

Chocolate Macaroons: Melt 2 squares unsweetened chocolate. Combine with condensed milk and vanilla before stirring into coconut mixture.

Condensed Milk

It is convenient to buy a can of condensed milk, but it is also expensive. You can easily make your own for about one-third the cost.

1 cup	*granulated sugar*	*250*	*mL*
1/3 cup	*water*	*75*	*mL*
1/3 cup	*butter or margarine*	*75*	*mL*
1 1/4 cups	*instant skim milk powder*	*300*	*mL*

In a small saucepan over medium heat, combine sugar, water and butter. Bring to a boil, stirring occasionally. Pour into blender container. Blend in milk powder, half at a time, until smooth, scraping sides as necessary. Store in refrigerator.

Makes 1 1/4 cups (300 mL) which is equivalent to a can of condensed milk.

Peanut Cookies

Crunchy and very tasty.

1 cup	butter or margarine*, softened	250	mL
1 cup	granulated sugar	250	mL
1 cup	brown sugar	250	mL
3	eggs	3	
2 tsp.	vanilla	10	mL
2 cups	all-purpose or whole-wheat flour	500	mL
2 tsp.	baking powder	10	mL
1/2 tsp.	baking soda	2	mL
1 1/2 cup	Spanish peanuts	375	mL
2 cups	corn flake cereal, crumbled	500	mL

Preheat oven to 350°F (180°C).

In a large bowl, cream butter and sugars. Beat in eggs and vanilla. Mix in flour, baking powder and baking soda. Mix in peanuts and cereal.

Bake a test cookie; see page 6 for directions.

Drop batter from a teaspoon onto greased cookie sheet. Bake for 10 minutes or until golden around the edges. Transfer to racks to cool.

Makes about 7 dozen.

* Use solid margarine; see page 4 for explanation.

More about solid margarine

If you have been accustomed to using soft margarine exclusively, here is a tip for keeping solid margarine on hand as well. Buy a 3-pound (1.36 kg) box of solid margarine individually wrapped in quarter-pound blocks. If refrigerator space is limited, store only 2 or 3 blocks in the refrigerator and freeze the rest. A quarter-pound block equals 1/2 cup (125 mL), a handy pre-measured amount, and you'll always have solid margarine on hand when you need it.

Golden Gems

This is an interesting soft oatmeal cookie recipe.
The finished cookies are an attractive golden colour
and there is no tomato soup flavour.

1 1/2 cups	all-purpose or whole wheat flour	375 mL
1 1/3 cups	granulated sugar	325 mL
1 tsp.	baking powder	5 mL
1/2 tsp.	baking soda	2 mL
2 tsp.	ground cinnamon	10 mL
1 tsp.	ground allspice	5 mL
1 cup	butter or margarine*, softened	250 mL
1	egg	1
1	can (284 mL) condensed tomato soup	1
2 cups	rolled oats	500 mL
1 cup	raisins	250 mL
1 cup	chopped walnuts (optional)	250 mL

Preheat oven to 350°F (180°C).

In a large bowl, stir together flour, sugar, baking powder, baking soda and spices. Add butter, egg and soup. Beat on medium speed for 2 minutes, scraping sides and bottom of bowl constantly. Stir in rolled oats, raisins and nuts.

Bake a test cookie; see page 6 for directions.

Drop batter from a teaspoon onto ungreased cookie sheet. Bake for 15 minutes or until lightly browned. Transfer to racks to cool.

Makes about 7 dozen.

* Use solid margarine; see page 4 for explanation.

For even baking

..make all cookies in a batch the same size.

Children's Cottage Cookie Cook Book

Chewy Bars

This spicy bar is a favourite with men. It is baked in "logs" — the finished product has a crust surrounding a chewy centre.

1/2 cup	butter or margarine*, softened	125	mL
1 cup	granulated sugar	250	mL
1	egg	1	
1/4 cup	molasses	50	mL
1 tsp.	baking soda	5	mL
1 tsp.	ground cinnamon	5	mL
1 tsp.	ground ginger	5	mL
1/2 tsp.	ground cloves	2	mL
1/2 cup	raisins	125	mL
1/4 cup	chopped candied cherries, pineapple or citron, or dried fruit such as apricots	50	mL
1/4 cup	chopped walnuts (optional)	50	mL
2 cups	all-purpose or whole wheat flour Granulated sugar	500	mL

Preheat oven to 400°F (200°C).

In a medium bowl, cream butter and sugar. Beat in egg, then molasses, baking soda and spices. Stir in raisins, fruit and walnuts. Blend in about three-quarters of the flour. Continue adding flour until dough is very stiff.

On a lightly-floured surface, working with one-quarter of the dough at a time, shape each portion into a log 12 inches (30 cm) long. Place on greased cookie sheet. Bake for 12 minutes or until lightly browned on bottom. There is not much change in colour of the top crust; do not overbake.

While still hot, sprinkle with a little granulated sugar and cut into diagonal bars. Transfer to racks to cool. Store in tightly covered container.

Makes about 4 dozen.

* Use solid margarine; see page 4 for explanation.

Good Cookies

The name says it all!

1/2 cup	butter or margarine*, softened	125	mL
1/2 cup	granulated sugar	125	mL
1/2 cup	brown sugar	125	mL
1	egg	1	
1/2 tsp.	baking powder	2	mL
1/2 tsp.	salt	2	mL
3/4 cup	all-purpose or whole wheat flour	175	mL
1 cup	rolled oats	250	mL
1 cup	flaked or shredded coconut	250	mL

Preheat oven to 350°F (180°C).

In a medium bowl, cream butter and sugars. Beat in egg, baking powder and salt. Blend in flour. Stir in rolled oats and coconut.

Bake a test cookie; see page 6 for directions.

Drop from a teaspoon onto greased cookie sheet. Bake for 12 minutes or until lightly browned. Transfer to racks to cool.

Makes 3 - 4 dozen.

* Use solid margarine; see page 4 for explanation.

Children's Cottage — love in action

The program at the Cottage is non-judgemental, non-threatening and confidential. It offers short-term relief to highly stressed parents in crisis situations. Services provided for parents include:
- *safe shelter for their children*
- *information and referral to agencies and services that may resolve the crisis*
- *non-judgemental and supportive atmosphere*
- *confidential help*

Soft Raisin Drops

Soft, moist, spicy, delicious!

2 cups	raisins	500	mL
1 cup	water	250	mL
1 tsp.	baking soda	5	mL
1 cup	butter or margarine*, softened	250	mL
2 cups	brown sugar	500	mL
3	eggs	3	
1 tsp.	vanilla	5	mL
3 1/2 cups	all-purpose flour	875	mL
1 tsp.	baking powder	5	mL
1/2 tsp.	salt	2	mL
1/2 tsp.	ground cinnamon	2	mL
1/4 tsp.	ground nutmeg	1	mL
1 cup	chopped walnuts	250	mL

Preheat oven to 375°F (190°C).

In a heavy saucepan, combine raisins and water. Boil gently for 5 minutes. Remove from heat. Stir in baking soda. Cool.

In a large bowl, cream butter and sugar. Beat in eggs and vanilla. Stir in flour. baking powder, salt and spices. Mix in cooled raisins with cooking liquid, and nuts.

Bake a test cookie; see page 6 for directions.

Drop batter from a teaspoon onto ungreased cookie sheet. Bake for 10 minutes or until brown on bottom. Transfer to racks to cool. Store with wax paper separating the layers to prevent cookies from sticking to each other.

Makes about 6 dozen.

* Use solid margarine; see page 4 for explanation.

Spatulas — cookies need them!

To ensure that cookies and bars remain intact, always use a metal spatula to remove them from pans; egg lifters work well for cookies, too.

Aunt Minnie Cookies

Great with coffee.

1 cup	butter or margarine*, softened	250 mL
1 cup	brown sugar	250 mL
2	eggs	2
2 tbsp.	milk	30 mL
1 tsp.	baking soda	5 mL
1 tsp.	baking powder	5 mL
1 tsp.	ground cinnamon	5 mL
1/4 tsp.	ground nutmeg	1 mL
1/4 tsp.	ground allspice	1 mL
1/4 tsp.	ground cloves	1 mL
1 cup	currants	250 mL
3 cups	all-purpose flour	750 mL

In a medium bowl, cream butter and sugar. Beat in eggs, milk, baking soda, baking powder and spices. Stir in currants. Mix in about two-thirds of the flour. Gradually stir in the remaining flour until dough is soft but not sticky. Chill for 3 hours.

Preheat oven to 350°F (180°C).

On a lightly-floured surface, roll dough to a thickness of 1/8 inch (3 mm). Cut into desired shapes and place on greased cookie sheet. Bake for 8 minutes or until lightly browned. Transfer to racks to cool.

Makes 8 - 12 dozen.

* Use solid margarine; see page 4 for explanation.

From a 1938 Cookbook—Advice for rolled cookies:

"Cookie dough should be kept as soft as can be handled. The softer the dough, the more tender the cookies. After mixing the dough, allow it to stand in a cold place* until thoroughly chilled. This chilling process will harden the fat, preventing stickiness; the moisture will be absorbed and the dough will not take up so much flour during the rolling process. Chilling is particularly necessary when making the mixtures containing a large amount of shortening."

* *In the '30s not everyone had an icebox or refrigerator.*

Oat Munchers

Everyone loved these.

1 cup	butter or margarine*, softened	250 mL
1/2 cup	granulated sugar	125 mL
1/2 cup	brown sugar	125 mL
2	eggs	2
1 tsp.	baking powder	5 mL
1/2 tsp.	baking soda	2 mL
1/2 tsp.	salt	2 mL
1 tsp.	vanilla	5 mL
2 cups	rolled oats	500 mL
1/2 cup	wheat germ	125 mL
1 1/2 cups	all-purpose or whole wheat flour	375 mL
3/4 cup	coconut	175 mL
1 cup	mixed peel, raisins, chopped prunes or nuts	250 mL

Preheat oven to 350°F (180°C).

In a large bowl, with electric mixer on low speed, cream butter and sugar. Add remaining ingredients in order given, mixing continuously.

Bake a test cookie; see page 6 for directions.

Drop heaping teaspoonfuls of batter, 1 1/2 inches (4 cm) apart, onto greased cookie sheet. Do not crowd. Bake for 10 minutes or until bottom edges are golden and top appears dry. Transfer to racks to cool.

Makes about 5 dozen.

* Use solid margarine; see page 4 for explanation.

Plumping Raisins

If raisins are dry and hard when added to cookie dough, they will be dry and hard after the cookies are baked. To "refresh" raisins, pour boiling water over them, let stand 5 minutes, drain and pat dry.

Honey Raisin Cookies

Soft, chewy, and easy to make.

1 cup	shortening, softened	250	mL
1 tsp.	baking soda	5	mL
1/2 tsp.	salt	2	mL
1 tsp.	ground cinnamon	5	mL
1 tsp.	ground cloves	5	mL
1/2 cup	brown sugar	125	mL
1/2 cup	honey	125	mL
3	eggs	3	
3 cups	all-purpose flour	750	mL
2 cups	raisins	500	mL
1/2 cup	walnuts, coarsely chopped	125	mL

Preheat oven to 350°F (180°C).

In a large bowl, cream shortening, baking soda, salt and spices. Add sugar and honey, blending thoroughly. Beat in eggs one at a time. Stir in flour, then raisins and nuts.

Bake a test cookie; see page 6 for directions.

Drop from a teaspoon onto greased cookie sheet. Bake for 12 minutes or until browned. Transfer to racks to cool.

Makes about 7 dozen.

Variation:

Replace half the raisins with 1 cup (250 mL) chopped dates or chocolate chips.

Cost-saving tip

Nuts are a nutritious addition to cookies, but some are also expensive. Don't overlook peanuts and sunflower seeds—they are usually more economical and offer taste variety since they are less-commonly used.

Apple Hermits

A moist cookie with nice flavour.

1/2 cup	shortening, softened	125	mL
1 cup	brown sugar	250	mL
2	eggs	2	
1/2 tsp.	baking soda	2	mL
1/2 tsp.	baking powder	2	mL
1/4 tsp.	salt	1	mL
1/2 tsp.	ground cinnamon	3	mL
1/2 cup	oatmeal	125	mL
1 cup	peeled coarsely grated apples	225	mL
1/2 cup	chopped walnuts	125	mL
1 3/4 cups	all-purpose or whole wheat flour	425	mL

Preheat oven to 375°F (190°C).

In a large bowl, cream shortening and sugar. Beat in eggs, baking soda, baking powder, salt and cinnamon. Stir in oatmeal and apple. Blend in flour, then nuts.

Bake a test cookie; see page 6 for directions.

Drop from a teaspoon onto ungreased cookie sheet. Bake for 12 minutes or until lightly browned. Transfer to racks to cool.

Makes about 2 dozen.

Frozen cookies defrost quickly; in fact, many taste just fine while they are still partially frozen.

Sesame Seed Cookies

*A light, tasty cookie — the hint of sesame
is a pleasant variation.*

2 tbsp.	sesame seeds	30	mL
1/4 cup	boiling water	60	mL
1/2 cup	butter or margarine*, softened	125	mL
1 cup	granulated sugar	250	mL
1	egg	1	
1 tsp.	baking powder	5	mL
1/2 tsp.	salt	2	mL
1 1/2 cups	all-purpose flour	375	mL

Spread sesame seeds on baking sheet. Bake at 350°F (180°C) for 15 minutes or until golden.

In a small bowl, combine sesame seeds and water.

In a medium bowl, cream butter and sugar until fluffy. Beat in egg, baking powder and salt. Blend in seeds and water. Stir in about three-quarters of the flour. Continue adding flour until rolling consistency is achieved. Chill for several hours.

Preheat oven to 350°F (180°C).

On a floured surface, roll dough one-quarter at a time to a thickness of 1/8 inch (3 mm). Using a pastry wheel or pizza cutter, cut dough into 2-inch (5 cm) squares. Place on greased cookie sheet. Bake for 10 minutes or until set and very lightly browned. Transfer to racks immediately to cool.

Makes about 5 dozen.

* Use solid margarine; see page 4 for explanation.

Dad's Cookies

Easy to make, nicely flavoured and chewy.
Transports well in lunches.

1 cup	butter or margarine*, softened	250 mL
1 cup	granulated sugar	250 mL
1/2 cup	brown sugar	125 mL
1	egg	1
1 tsp.	vanilla	5 mL
1 tsp.	baking powder	5 mL
1 tsp.	baking soda	5 mL
1/2 tsp.	salt	2 mL
1 1/2 cups	all-purpose or whole wheat flour	375 mL
1 1/2 cups	rolled oats	375 mL
1/2 cup	coconut	125 mL
1/2 cup	crushed crispy rice cereal	125 mL

Preheat oven to 375°F (190°C).

In a large bowl, cream butter and sugars. Beat in egg, vanilla, baking powder, baking soda and salt. Stir in flour. Mix in rolled oats, coconut and crushed cereal.

Bake a test cookie; see page 6 for directions.

Form dough into balls about 1 inch (2.5 cm) in diameter. Place on greased cookie sheet and flatten with a fork. Bake for 15 minutes or until slightly browned around the edges. Transfer to racks to cool.

Makes 3 - 4 dozen.

* Use solid margarine; see page 4 for explanation.

*To make a 1-inch (2.5 cm) ball of dough,
use approximately 1 tablespoon (15 mL).*

Lemonade Cookies

Kids love them.

1 cup	butter or margarine*, softened	250 mL
1 1/4 cups	granulated sugar, divided	300 mL
2	eggs	2
1 tsp.	baking soda	5 mL
3 cups	all-purpose flour	750 mL
1	can (178 mL) frozen lemonade concentrate, thawed and divided	1

Preheat oven to 375°F (190°C).

In a large bowl, cream butter and 1 cup (250 mL) of the sugar. Beat in eggs and baking soda. Add flour to creamed mixture alternately with 1/2 cup (125 mL) of the lemonade concentrate.

Bake a test cookie; see page 6 for directions.

Drop batter from a teaspoon 2 inches (5 cm) apart onto ungreased cookie sheet. Bake 8 minutes or until edges are lightly browned. Brush lightly with remaining lemonade concentrate and sprinkle with remaining sugar. Transfer to racks to cool.

Makes about 6 dozen.

* Use solid margarine; see page 4 for explanation.

True Story

The father of a young family said grace before each meal—the one which begins "Our Father, we thank You for this food." Three-year-old Ginny would bow her head demurely, appearing to understand what was being said. Then one day this illusion was shattered when she turned to her father and asked, "Dad, how come we always thank you when it's Mom who does the cookin'?"

Peanut Butter Balls

An unbaked treat.

1/2 cup	graham wafer crumbs	125	mL
1 cup	icing sugar	250	mL
1 cup	crunchy peanut butter	250	mL
1 cup	chocolate chips	250	mL
1/2 cup	instant skim milk powder	125	mL
3 tbsp.	water	45	mL
	Graham wafer crumbs		
	or coconut (optional)		

In a medium bowl, thoroughly combine all ingredients except the extra crumbs or coconut.

Shape mixture into 1-inch (2.5 cm) balls. Mixture should be damp enough to hold together. If too dry, add a little extra water; if too sticky, add a few more crumbs. Roll in extra crumbs or coconut, if desired. Refrigerate until firm.

Makes 2 - 3 dozen.

Butterscotch Oaties

An immediate family favourite!

1 cup	butterscotch chips	250	mL
3/4 cup	butter or margarine*	175	mL
2 tbsp.	boiling water	25	mL
1 tsp.	baking soda	5	mL
1 cup	all-purpose flour	250	mL
3/4 cup	granulated sugar	175	mL
2 cups	rolled oats	500	mL

Preheat oven to 350°F (180°C).

In a double boiler, or medium bowl placed over hot water, melt butterscotch chips and butter.** Remove from heat.

In a small dish, combine boiling water and baking soda. Stir into butterscotch mixture. Thoroughly blend in flour and sugar. Mix in rolled oats.

Bake a test cookie; see page 6 for directions.

Drop batter from a teaspoon onto ungreased cookie sheet. Bake for 12 minutes or until nicely browned. Cool on baking sheet for 2 minutes, then transfer to racks to cool.

Makes about 5 dozen.

* Use solid margarine; see page 4 for explanation.
** This can also be done in the microwave oven.

Greasing cookie sheets is unnecessary when the cookie dough contains a lot of shortening, but you can always put a light film of butter or shortening on the pans if you have any question. Use your fingers or a piece of crumpled paper towel to grease the pans, dipping it into the soft butter or vegetable shortening and running it lightly over the pans. Cookie sheets don't need washing or regreasing between batches; just wipe off any crumbs.

Cracker Jack Cookies

A good family and lunchbox cookie.

1 cup	butter or margarine*, softened	250	mL
1 cup	brown sugar	250	mL
1 cup	granulated sugar	250	mL
2	eggs	2	
2 tsp.	vanilla	10	mL
1 tsp.	baking powder	5	mL
1 tsp.	baking soda	5	mL
1 1/2 cups	all-purpose or whole wheat flour	375	mL
2 cups	rolled oats	500	mL
1 cup	coconut	250	mL
2 cups	crispy rice cereal	500	mL
1/2 cup	roasted peanuts (optional)	125	mL

Preheat oven to 350°F (180°C).

In a large bowl, cream butter and sugars. Beat in eggs, vanilla, baking powder and baking soda. Stir in flour. Mix in rolled oats, coconut and cereal. Stir in peanuts.

Bake a test cookie; see page 6 for directions.

Drop batter from a teaspoon onto ungreased cookie sheet. Bake for 11 minutes or until light golden brown. Transfer to racks to cool.

Makes about 4 dozen.

* Use solid margarine; see page 4 for explanation.

Peanut Crunchies

Our home economist's comment: "Rather expensive, but a real hit with everyone who tasted them."

3 cups	chocolate chips	750 mL
1 cup	butterscotch chips	250 mL
3 cups	roasted peanuts	750 mL
3 cups	crushed potato chips	750 mL

In a large double boiler, or bowl placed over hot water, melt chocolate and butterscotch chips. Pour over peanuts and potato chips; combine thoroughly.

Drop mixture from a teaspoon onto cookie sheet covered with wax paper. Refrigerate until firm, approximately 30 minutes. Store in refrigerator.

Makes about 5 dozen.

Cost saving tip

Bulk buying is usually economical. Chocolate chips, for instance, are one-third the price when bought in bulk.

Peanut Butter Cookies

Always a favourite.

1/2 cup	butter or margarine*, softened	125	mL
1/2 cup	granulated sugar	125	mL
1/2 cup	brown sugar	125	mL
1	egg	1	
1/2 tsp.	vanilla	2	mL
1/2 cup	smooth or crunchy peanut butter	125	mL
1/2 tsp.	baking soda	2	mL
1/4 tsp.	salt	1	mL
1 1/4 cups	all-purpose or whole wheat flour	300	mL

Preheat oven to 350°F (180°C).

In a medium bowl, cream butter and sugars. Beat in egg, vanilla, peanut butter, baking soda and salt. Stir in flour.

Bake a test cookie; see page 6 for directions.

Roll dough into 1-inch (2.5 cm) balls. Place on lightly greased cookie sheet and flatten with a fork. Bake for 10 minutes or until nicely browned. Transfer to racks to cool.

Makes 3 - 4 dozen.

* Use solid margarine; see page 4 for explanation.

Non-stick peanut butter

When measuring peanut butter, oil the cup lightly first—peanut butter then slips out easily. The no-fuss way of oiling a measuring cup is to pour vegetable oil into the clean cup, then pour it back into the bottle. The oil that clings to the cup is just the right amount to do the job.

Classic Chocolate Chip Cookies

What's to say?!

1/2 cup	butter	125	mL
1/2 cup	shortening	125	mL
1 cup	granulated sugar	250	mL
1/2 cup	brown sugar	125	mL
2	eggs	2	
2 tsp.	vanilla	10	mL
1 tsp.	baking soda	5	mL
1/2 tsp.	salt	2	mL
2 cups	all-purpose or whole wheat flour	500	mL
1 cup	chopped walnuts or pecans	250	mL
2 cups	chocolate chips	500	mL

In a large bowl, cream butter and shortening. Gradually add sugars, creaming thoroughly. Beat in eggs, vanilla, baking soda and salt. Stir in flour. Mix in nuts and chocolate chips. Chill dough for a few minutes or let stand at cool room temperature for about 30 minutes; this allows the dough to firm up, and cookies will keep their shape better during baking.

Preheat oven to 375°F (190°C).

Bake a test cookie; see page 6 for directions.

Drop dough from a teaspoon onto lightly greased cookie sheet. With your hands, flatten cookies slightly and smooth edges to give an even thickness of about 1/2-inch (1 cm).

For a soft chewy cookie, bake for 8 minutes or until cookies are golden brown around edges and still slightly underbaked in centre. Remove from oven and let stand on cookie sheet for 5 minutes. Cookies will continue to brown a bit and wrinkle slightly in centre. Transfer to racks to cool. For a crisp cookie, bake 11 minutes or until golden brown.

Makes about 4 dozen.

Variations:

Chocolate Chunk Cookies: Use 8 ounces (250 g) chopped semisweet squares or bittersweet chocolate bars instead of packaged chocolate chips. Chocolate should be at warm room temperature for easy chopping (or warm it very slightly, without melting, for a few seconds in microwave oven or warm conventional oven). With sharp knife, cut chocolate into pieces about 1/2-inch (1 cm) in size.

White Chocolate Nut Cookies: Use 8 squares white baking chocolate, chopped as directed above, instead of chocolate chips. Instead of walnuts or pecans, use macadamia nuts, hazelnuts or almonds.

Chocolate Chip Bars: Instead of making individual cookies, press dough into greased 10 x 15 (25 x 40 cm) jelly roll pan. Bake at 375°F (190°C) for 20 minutes or until nicely browned and still slightly underbaked in centre.

What we've learned about chocolate chip cookies

- People love them!
- Chocolate in any form, shape or size is acceptable—very large chunks are particularly popular.
- Some people like chewy chocolate chip cookies, and some like them crisp. So...chewy cookie lovers bake theirs until barely browned—crisp cookie lovers bake theirs until golden.

Big and Chewy
Chocolate Chippers

Big batch, big chocolate chunks, big taste.

2 cups	butter or margarine*, softened	500	mL
2 cups	granulated sugar	500	mL
2 cups	brown sugar	500	mL
4	eggs	4	
2 tsp.	vanilla	10	mL
2 tsp.	baking powder	10	mL
2 tsp.	baking soda	10	mL
1 tsp.	salt	5	mL
5 cups	rolled oats	1.25	L
4 cups	all-purpose or whole wheat flour	1	L
2 cups	chocolate chips	500	mL
2	milk chocolate bars (100 g each), cut in large chunks	2	
3 cups	chopped nuts	750	mL

Preheat oven to 375°F (190°C).

In a very large bowl, cream butter. Gradually add sugars, creaming thoroughly. Beat in eggs, vanilla, baking powder, baking soda and salt.

Grind rolled oats to a powder in blender or food processor, working with a third of the total amount at a time. Measure the flour; remove about 1/2 cup (125 mL) and set aside. Add remaining flour to powdered oats; stir to combine well. Stir into creamed mixture. Dough should be very thick; add reserved flour if needed.

In another bowl, combine the chocolate chips, chocolate chunks and nuts. Add to dough and mix in.

Bake a test cookie. It should spread slightly. See page 6 for directions.

Shape dough into balls the size of a golf ball. Place on ungreased baking sheet and press gently. Bake for 10 minutes or until cookies are golden on the bottom and still pale on top. Let stand for 2 - 3 minutes before transferring to racks to cool.

Makes 9 - 10 dozen. This recipe can be easily halved.

* Use solid margarine; see page 4 for explanation.

The Monster Batch

This recipe makes a large batch of exceptionally tasty cookies. The home economist who tested this recipe took about 15 dozen to a kids' sporting club event — they disappeared quickly.

1 cup	butter or margarine*, softened	250 mL
3 cups	peanut butter	750 mL
2 cups	granulated sugar	500 mL
2 1/2 cups	brown sugar	625 mL
6	eggs	6
1 tsp.	vanilla	5 mL
4 tsp.	baking soda	20 mL
5 cups	oatmeal	1.25 L
5 cups	crispy rice cereal	1.25 L
1 cup	chocolate chips	250 mL
2	packages (125 g each) smarties	2

Preheat oven to 350°F (180°C).

In a very large bowl, cream butter, peanut butter and sugars. Beat in eggs, vanilla and baking soda. Stir in oatmeal, cereal and chocolate chips.

Form dough into 1-inch (2.5 cm) balls. Place on ungreased cookie sheet. Press a smartie in the centre of each. Bake for 8 minutes or until golden brown. Cookie will still be soft in centre; it hardens as it cools. Let cool slightly. Transfer to racks to finish cooling.

Makes 17 - 18 dozen.

Yes, this recipe has no flour!

* Use solid margarine; see page 4 for explanation.

Cookie Pans

For proper browning of cookies, the pans need to be shallow. Use either rimless cookie sheets or pans with shallow edges, such as jelly roll pans or sheets designed especially for cookies. Do not use cake pans; the high sides prevent cookies from browning sufficiently.

Chewy Oatmeal Cookies

A wonderful, chewy cookie — just like Grandma used to make!

1 3/4 cups	rolled oats	425 mL
1 1/2 cups	all-purpose or whole wheat flour	375 mL
1 cup	granulated sugar	250 mL
1/2 tsp.	baking soda	2 mL
1/2 tsp.	salt	2 mL
1 tsp.	ground cinnamon	5 mL
1	egg	1
1/4 cup	milk	60 mL
1 tbsp.	molasses	15 mL
1/2 cup	melted shortening	125 mL
1/2 cup	melted butter	125 mL
1/2 cup	raisins	125 mL

Preheat oven to 350°F (180°C).

In a large bowl, combine dry ingredients.

In a medium bowl, beat egg. Blend in milk, molasses, shortening and butter. Add to dry ingredients, combining thoroughly. Stir in raisins. Drop from a teaspoon onto ungreased cookie sheet. Bake for 12 minutes or until slightly browned. Transfer to racks to cool.

Makes about 4 dozen.

Power-pack your favourite recipes

The nutritional value of any cookie can be increased by increasing the quantity of nuts, sunflower seeds or dried fruit. Some recipes can easily accommodate the addition of wheat germ or skim milk powder. Experiment to see what you can create.

Rolled Oat Drop Cookies

Good with either chocolate chips or raisins.

1 cup	shortening, softened	250 mL
1 cup	granulated sugar	250 mL
2	eggs	2
2 tbsp.	milk	30 mL
1 tsp.	baking powder	5 mL
1/2 tsp.	salt	2 mL
1 tsp.	ground cinnamon	5 mL
1 tsp.	ground nutmeg	5 mL
1/4 tsp.	ground cloves	1 mL
2 cups	all-purpose or whole wheat flour	500 mL
2 cups	rolled oats	500 mL
1 cup	raisins or chocolate chips	250 mL
1 cup	chopped nuts	250 mL

Preheat oven to 375°F (190°C).

In a large bowl, cream shortening and sugar. Beat in eggs, milk, baking powder, salt and spices. Stir in flour. Mix in rolled oats, raisins and nuts.

Bake a test cookie; see page 6 for directions.

Drop batter from a teaspoon onto ungreased cookie sheet. Bake for 12 minutes or until light brown on the bottom. Transfer to racks to cool.

Makes about 5 dozen.

If you like cookies chewy and slightly soft, keep them in the oven for a shorter time than called for; leave them in longer if you want them to be very crisp.

Chocolate Chip Date Bars

Easy and very good.

1/3 cup	butter or margarine*, softened	75 mL
1 cup	brown sugar	250 mL
1	egg	1
1 tsp.	vanilla	5 mL
1/2 tsp.	baking powder	2 mL
1/4 tsp.	baking soda	1 mL
1/4 tsp.	salt	1 mL
1 cup	all-purpose or whole wheat flour	250 mL
1 cup	chocolate chips	250 mL
1 cup	chopped walnuts (optional)	250 mL
1/2 cup	chopped dates	125 mL

Preheat oven to 350°F (180°C).

In a medium bowl, cream butter and sugar. Beat in egg, vanilla, baking powder, baking soda and salt. Stir in flour. Mix in chocolate chips, walnuts and dates.

Press in well-greased 9-inch (22 cm) square baking pan. Bake for 20 minutes or until toothpick inserted in centre comes out clean.

Makes about 2 dozen.

* Use solid margarine; see page 4 for explanation.

Children's Cottage—love in action

The Cottage provides support for parents who feel less able to care for their children for a variety of reasons—sudden illness or hospitalization, marital conflict, housing problems, fear of hurting or neglecting their children, trouble coping with a newborn, financial crisis, or feelings of depression and isolation.

Almond Crunch

Amazingly simple...and so good!

	Whole graham wafers	
1	package (100 g) flaked or slivered almonds	1
1 cup	butter	250 mL
3/4 cup	brown sugar	175 mL

Preheat oven to 350°F (180°C).

Place a single layer of graham wafers in an ungreased 9 x 13-inch (22 x 34 cm) baking pan, making sure they fit snugly. Sprinkle with almonds.

In a heavy saucepan over medium heat, cook and stir butter and sugar until mixture comes to a boil. Boil gently for 3 minutes. Drizzle over almond-covered wafers, spreading evenly. Bake for 8 minutes or until mixture is bubbly. Cut into bars while still slightly warm.

Makes about 3 dozen.

Variation:

Almond Roca Bars: Sprinkle only half the almonds over graham wafers. Continue as directed. When removed from oven, sprinkle immediately with 1 package (300 g) chocolate chips. When chocolate melts, spread gently. Sprinkle with remaining almonds. Refrigerate for about 30 minutes to set chocolate. Cut into bars. Store at room temperature.

Cost-saving tip

Ingredients bought in bulk are often less expensive. When using bulk products, refer to "How Much in a Package?" on page 9 to know the quantity required when a recipe calls for a particular package size.

Jam Bars

Easy to make, with very good flavour.
Add a personal touch by using the jam of your choice.

1/2 cup	butter or margarine*, softened	125	mL
1 cup	brown sugar	250	mL
1/2 tsp.	baking soda	2	mL
1/2 tsp.	salt	2	mL
1 1/2 cups	all-purpose flour	375	mL
1 1/2 cups	rolled oats	375	mL
1/4 cup	water	60	mL
1 tsp.	lemon juice	5	mL
2/3 cup	jam**	150	mL

Preheat oven to 350°F (180°C).

In a medium bowl, cream butter, sugar, baking soda and salt until fluffy. Stir in flour. Work in rolled oats and water; mixture will be crumbly. Firmly pat half into greased 9 x 13-inch (22 x 34 cm) baking pan.

Stir lemon juice into jam. Spread over base. Sprinkle with remaining crumb mixture. Bake for 25 minutes or until golden brown. Cool and cut into bars.

Makes about 3 dozen.

* Use solid margarine; see page 4 for explanation.
** If jam is very thick, increase lemon juice to 1 1/2 teaspoons. Do not use freezer jam; it has a different consistency and may not bake well.

Variation:

Spread base with several types of jam. A good way to use up those "dribs and drabs" that seem to stay at the bottom of jam jars.

Don't have a 9 x 13-inch pan?

Use two 8-inch square pans.

Applesauce Bars

Easy, spicy, moist, delicious.

1/2 cup	butter or margarine*, softened	125	mL
2/3 cup	brown sugar	150	mL
1/3 cup	liquid honey	75	mL
2 tsp.	baking soda	10	mL
1 tsp.	salt	5	mL
1 tsp.	ground cinnamon	5	mL
1/4 tsp.	ground nutmeg	1	mL
1/4 tsp.	ground cloves	1	mL
1 1/2 cups	applesauce	375	mL
2 1/2 cups	all-purpose or whole wheat flour	625	mL
1 cup	raisins	250	mL
1/2 cup	chopped nuts (optional) Glaze	125	mL

Preheat oven to 350°F (180°C).

In a large bowl, cream butter, sugar, honey, baking soda, salt and spices. Beat in applesauce. Blend in flour. Stir in raisins and nuts. Spread in greased 10 x 15-inch (25 x 40 cm) jelly roll pan. Bake for 25 minutes or until centre springs back when lightly touched. While hot, spread with Glaze.

Glaze

1/2 cup	icing sugar	125	mL
1 tbsp.	hot coffee or water	15	mL

In a small bowl, combine ingredients until smooth.

Makes 3 - 4 dozen.

* Use solid margarine; see page 4 for explanation.

Poppy Seed Poppers

This bar is moist, chewy and very good tasting — nice addition to any cookie plate.

1 1/4 cups	granulated sugar	300	mL
1 1/2 cups	all-purpose flour	375	mL
1 tsp.	baking powder	5	mL
1/4 tsp.	baking soda	1	mL
1/4 tsp.	salt	1	mL
1/2 cup	butter, melted	125	mL
1/3 cup	liquid honey	75	mL
2	eggs	2	
2 tbsp.	milk	30	mL
1 1/2 tsp.	vanilla	7	mL
1/8 tsp.	almond extract	0.5	mL
1 cup	shredded coconut	250	mL
1/3 cup	poppy seeds	75	mL

Preheat oven to 350°F (180°C).

In a medium bowl, combine sugar, flour, baking powder, baking soda and salt.

In another bowl, combine butter, honey, eggs, milk, vanilla and almond extract. Add to dry ingredients, mixing until smooth. Stir in coconut and poppy seeds. Spread in greased 9 x 13 inch (22 x 34 cm) baking pan. Bake for 30 minutes or until lightly browned.

Makes about 4 dozen.

Spicy Sesame Squares

Flavourful, easy, and chewy describes this square.

1/4 cup	sesame seeds	50	mL
1	egg	1	
3/4 cup	brown sugar	175	mL
3 tbsp.	melted butter	50	mL
1/2 cup	all-purpose or whole wheat flour	125	mL
1/4 tsp.	baking soda	1	mL
1/4 tsp.	salt	1	mL
1/4 tsp.	ground allspice	1	mL
1/4 tsp.	ground cardamom* or cinnamon	1	mL
1/4 tsp.	ground nutmeg	1	mL

Preheat oven to 350°F (180°C).

Spread sesame seeds in large flat pan. Toast in the oven for 10 minutes or until golden. Sprinkle half of toasted seeds evenly over bottom of greased 8-inch (20 cm) square baking pan.

In a medium bowl, beat egg. Gradually beat in sugar. Blend in melted butter. Stir in remaining ingredients, blending thoroughly. Spoon batter into baking pan on top of seeds. Spread evenly and carefully. Sprinkle remaining seeds on top. Bake for 25 minutes or until top springs back when lightly touched but centre is still chewy.

Makes about 2 dozen.

* May be increased to 1/2 teaspoon (2 mL) for those who enjoy this distinctive flavour.

Golden Harvest Bars

These bars are tasty and moist.
A good way to use that bit of leftover pumpkin.

2	eggs	2
3/4 cup	brown sugar	175 mL
1/2 cup	cooked mashed pumpkin	125 mL
1/4 cup	vegetable oil	50 mL
1/2 tsp.	vanilla	2 mL
3/4 cup	all-purpose or whole wheat flour	175 mL
1 tsp.	baking powder	5 mL
1/2 tsp.	salt	2 mL
1/2 tsp.	ground cinnamon	2 mL
1/2 tsp.	ground nutmeg	2 mL
2 tsp.	grated orange peel	10 mL
1/2 cup	chopped dates or raisins	125 mL
1/2 cup	chopped nuts	125 mL
	Icing sugar	

Preheat oven to 350°F (180°C).

In a medium bowl, beat eggs. Add sugar, pumpkin, oil and vanilla; beat well. Thoroughly stir in flour, baking powder, salt, spices and orange peel. Mix in dates and nuts. Spread batter in greased 9-inch (22 cm) square baking pan. Bake for 25 minutes or until top springs back when lightly touched. Cool, then dust with icing sugar.

Makes about 2 dozen.

Variation:

Omit dusting with icing sugar. Frost with simple butter icing and sprinkle with grated orange rind.

Pineapple Preserve Bars

Excellent pineapple flavour in this rather unusual bar.

3/4 cup	butter or margarine*, softened	175	mL
1 cup	granulated sugar	250	mL
1	egg	1	
1/2 cup	pineapple preserves or jam	125	mL
2 cup	all-purpose or whole wheat flour	500	mL
1 tsp.	baking soda	5	mL
1/2 tsp	salt	2	mL
1/2 cup	chopped nuts	125	mL
	Pineapple Frosting (optional)		

Preheat oven to 350°F (180°C).

In a medium bowl, cream butter and sugar until fluffy. Beat in egg and preserves. Stir in flour, baking soda and salt. Mix in nuts. Spread in greased 9 x 13-inch (22 x 34 cm) baking pan. Bake for 30 minutes or until browned. Cool slightly, then spread with Pineapple Frosting, if desired.

Pineapple Frosting

1 1/4 cups	icing sugar	300	mL
2 tbsp.	butter or margarine, softened	25	mL
2 tbsp.	pineapple preserves or jam	25	mL
1 tbsp.	milk	15	mL

In a small bowl, combine sugar, butter and preserves until smooth. Stir in enough of the milk to achieve spreading consistency.

Makes about 3 dozen.

* Use solid margarine; see page 4 for explanation.

Crabapple Squares

The cheese gives these squares a wonderful flavour.

3/4 cup	butter, softened	175	mL
1/4 cup	granulated sugar	50	mL
1 1/2 cups	all-purpose or whole wheat flour	375	mL
1/8 tsp.	salt	0.5	mL
1 cup	grated cheddar cheese	250	mL
1/2 cup	finely chopped pecans	125	mL
1 cup	crabapple jelly	250	mL

Preheat oven to 350°F (180°C).

In a medium bowl, cream butter and sugar. Stir in flour and salt. Mix in cheese and pecans. Mixture will be crumbly.

Press half of mixture into a greased 9-inch (22 cm) square baking pan. Spread jelly evenly over base. Sprinkle remaining crumb mixture on top. Bake for 30 minutes or until golden brown.

Makes about 2 dozen.

Chocolate Revel Bars

A first cousin of the old favourite Matrimonial Cake (Date Squares) — a creamy chocolate mixture replaces the date filling.

1 cup	butter or margarine*, softened	250 mL
2 cups	brown sugar	500 mL
2	eggs	2
2 tsp.	vanilla	10 mL
3 cups	rolled oats	750 mL
2 1/2 cups	all-purpose or whole wheat flour	625 mL
1 tsp.	baking soda	5 mL
1 tsp.	salt	5 mL
1	can (300 mL) sweetened condensed milk	1
1	package (300 g) chocolate chips	1
2 tbsp.	butter or margarine	25 mL
1 cup	chopped walnuts	250 mL
2 tsp.	vanilla	10 mL

Preheat oven to 350°F (180°C).

In a large bowl, cream 1 cup (250 mL) butter with sugar until fluffy. Beat in eggs and 2 teaspoons (10 mL) vanilla. Stir in oats, flour, baking soda and salt.

In a heavy saucepan over low heat, combine milk, chocolate chips and the 2 tablespoons (25 mL) butter. Heat, stirring frequently, until smooth. Remove from heat. Stir in nuts and 2 teaspoons (10 mL) vanilla.

Press two-thirds of the oat mixture into ungreased 10 x 15-inch (25 x 40 cm) jelly roll pan. Spread chocolate mixture over oat layer. Sprinkle with remaining oat mixture. Bake for 25 minutes or until lightly browned on top.

Makes about 5 dozen.

* Use solid margarine; see page 4 for explanation.

 If no one sees you eat a cookie, it has no calories.

Fudge Brownies

This reliable old favourite includes
a number of interesting variations.

1/2 cup	butter or margarine*, melted	125 mL
1 cup	granulated sugar	250 mL
1/4 cup	cocoa	60 mL
2	eggs	2
2/3 cup	all-purpose flour	150 mL
1/2 cup	chopped nuts, dates, raisins or coconut	125 mL
	Chocolate Icing (optional)	

Preheat oven to 375°F (190°C).

In a medium bowl, combine butter, sugar and cocoa. Add eggs, blending thoroughly. Stir in flour. Mix in nuts, fruit or coconut. Spread in greased 8-inch (20 cm) square baking pan. Bake for 30 minutes or until top springs back when touched lightly with finger and sides have begun to pull away from pan. Ice while hot with Chocolate Icing.

Chocolate Icing

3/4 cup	icing sugar	175 mL
2 tbsp.	cocoa	25 mL
2 tbsp.	butter or margarine, softened	25 mL
	Boiling water	

In a small bowl, combine icing sugar, cocoa, butter and approximately 2 tablespoons (25 mL) boiling water. Add a bit more water, if necessary, to make icing of spreading consistency.

Makes about 2 dozen.

Variations:

Rocky Mountain Frosting As soon as brownies are removed from oven, cover entire surface with plain or coloured miniature marshmallows. Make Chocolate Icing, reducing icing sugar to 1/2 cup (125 mL) and other ingredients proportionately, adding enough boiling water to make icing slightly runny. Drizzle over marshmallows.

Chocolate Pastel Frosting Omit the nuts, raisins, dates or coconut. Frost with raspberry, strawberry or orange frosting made by combining 1 cup (250 mL) icing sugar, 2 tablespoons (25 mL) butter or margarine, and enough boiling water to make frosting of spreading consistency. Add strawberry, raspberry or orange flavouring to taste. Use red food colouring to tint the strawberry and raspberry icings a delicate pink. To colour the orange-flavoured frosting, combine a little red and yellow food colouring in a small dish until desired orange colour is reached. Add enough to frosting to give desired orange shade. Decorate with chocolate sprinkles or melt 1 square semi-sweet chocolate and drizzle over coloured icing in a lacy pattern.

˚ Use solid margarine; see page 4 for explanation.

For satiny smooth icing

Boiling water makes an amazing difference in icing. It cooks the raw starch in the icing sugar, giving better flavour and a satiny smooth texture. If you haven't experienced this, it's worth a try.

Marshmallow Crispies

A long-time favourite with folks of all ages.

1/4 cup	butter or margarine*	50	mL
15	marshmallows (regular size)	15	
1/2 tsp.	vanilla	2	mL
3 1/2 cups	crispy rice cereal	875	mL

In a large saucepan over low heat, melt butter. Add marshmallows. Cook and stir until melted. Remove from heat. Blend in vanilla. Stir in cereal, mixing thoroughly. Press into greased 8-inch (20 cm) square baking pan.

Makes about 2 dozen.

* Use solid margarine; see page 4 for explanation.

Peanut Butter Candy Bars

A popular recipe with our tasters.

2/3 cup	butter or margarine*, softened	150 mL
1/2 cup	corn syrup	125 mL
1 cup	brown sugar	250 mL
4 cups	rolled oats	1 L
1 cup	chocolate chips, melted	250 mL
2 cups	crunchy peanut butter	500 mL

Preheat oven to 350°F (180°C).

In a large bowl, cream butter, syrup and sugar. Stir in rolled oats. With moistened hands, press mixture firmly into a well-greased 10 x 15-inch (25 x 40 cm) jelly roll pan. Bake for 15 minutes or until lightly browned. Cool slightly.

In a medium bowl, combine melted chocolate and peanut butter. Spread on cookie base. Cut into bars while warm. Refrigerate for 1 hour or until topping is set. Store in a cool place.

Makes about 5 dozen.

* Use solid margarine; see page 4 for explanation.

Puffed Wheat Squares

Quick, easy and popular.

8 cups	puffed wheat cereal	2 L
1/3 cup	butter or margarine*	75 mL
1/2 cup	corn syrup	125 mL
3/4 cup	brown sugar	175 mL
2 tbsp.	cocoa	25 mL

Measure puffed wheat into large bowl.

In a heavy saucepan over medium heat, combine butter, syrup, sugar and cocoa. Heat, stirring frequently, until sugar is dissolved and mixture comes to a full boil. Pour over puffed wheat. Mix thoroughly. Press into greased 9 x 13-inch (22 x 34 cm) baking pan. Let stand at room temperature until set, about 30 minutes.

Makes 2 - 3 dozen.

* Use solid margarine; see page 4 for explanation.

Butter Tart Bars

Butter tarts made easy.

1 1/2 cups	all-purpose flour	375	mL
2 tbsp.	icing sugar	25	mL
1/2 cup	butter or margarine[*]	125	mL
2	eggs	2	
1 1/2 cups	brown sugar	375	mL
1/2 cup	butter or margarine[*], melted	125	mL
1 tsp.	vinegar	5	mL
1 tsp.	vanilla	5	mL
1 cup	raisins	250	mL
1/2 cup	chopped walnuts (optional)[**]	125	mL

Preheat oven to 350°F (180°C).

In a medium bowl, combine flour and icing sugar. Using a pastry blender or two knives, cut in butter until mixture resembles coarse crumbs. Press into ungreased 9-inch (22 cm) square baking pan. Bake for 10 minutes.

In the same bowl, beat eggs. Stir in sugar, butter, vinegar and vanilla. Mix in raisins and nuts. Spread over base. Bake for 35 minutes or until set.

Makes 2 - 3 dozen.

[*] Use solid margarine; see page 4 for explanation.
[**] If omitting walnuts, increase raisins to 1 1/2 cups (375 mL).

Almond Granola Bars

Our tasters were wildly enthusiastic about this bar!

1/4 cup	butter or margarine*, melted	50 mL
1/3 cup	brown sugar	75 mL
1/4 tsp.	salt	1 mL
1 tbsp.	honey	15 mL
1 tbsp.	corn syrup	15 mL
1 tsp.	vanilla	5 mL
1 cup	granola	250 mL
1/2 cup	coconut	125 mL
1/2 cup	slivered almonds	125 mL
1/4 cup	ground almonds	50 mL
1/2 cup	chocolate chips, melted (optional)	125 mL
2 tbsp.	crunchy peanut butter (optional)	25 mL

Preheat oven to 350°F (180°C).

In a medium bowl, thoroughly combine butter, sugar, salt, honey, corn syrup and vanilla. Stir in granola, coconut and almonds, mixing until well coated. Press into greased 8-inch (20 cm) square baking pan. Bake for 15 minutes or until browned around edges. Cool.

Combine melted chocolate chips and peanut butter. Spread on baked bars. Chill for at least an hour before cutting. Cut with a sharp knife and lift out with a spatula.

Makes about 2 dozen.

* Use solid margarine; see page 4 for explanation.

Oldies
...but Goodies

The recipes in this section came from our collection of old cookbooks. Some intrigued us because we had never heard of them before. Others were long-forgotten treats that brought back memories when we tasted them. All, we decided, were oldies but goodies.

Dropped

Shaped

Rolled

Unbaked

Bar

Oldies...but Goodies

1. Fig Bars *p. 143*
2. Cherry Surprises *p. 144*
3. Date Ribbons *p. 145*
4. Carrot Cookies *p. 146*
5. Snappy Turtles *p. 147*

Fig Bars

This recipe came from a 1932 cookbook — truly an oldie and a goodie. It was popular with our tasters, including folks who normally disliked both figs and/or the store-bought version of this bar. Dough requires chilling.

1 cup	butter or margarine*, softened	250	mL
2 cups	brown sugar	500	mL
3	eggs	3	
1 tsp.	vanilla	5	mL
1/8 tsp.	salt	0.5	mL
1 tsp.	baking soda	5	mL
3 1/2 cups	whole wheat flour	875	mL
1/2 cup	all-purpose flour	125	mL
	Fig Jam		

In a large bowl, cream butter and sugar. Beat in eggs, vanilla, salt and baking soda. Stir in about three-quarters of the flour. Continue adding flour until dough is moderately stiff. Chill for several hours or overnight.

Preheat oven to 375°F (190°C).

On a lightly floured surface, working with one-third of the dough at a time, roll into a strip about 3 x 24 inches (8 x 60 cm). Put a mound of fig jam down centre of each strip. Gently fold edges of dough to meet in the centre, enclosing the filling. Press lightly to seal dough. Cut into bars 1 - 2 inches (2.5 - 5 cm) long. Carefully place seam-side-down on lightly greased cookie sheet. Bake for 15 minutes or until browned. Transfer to racks to cool.

Fig Jam

2 2/3 cups	cut-up figs**	650	mL
1 cup	granulated sugar	250	mL
1 cup	hot water	250	mL
1 tbsp.	lemon juice	15	mL

In a heavy saucepan over medium heat, cook and stir until mixture is thick and smooth. (A hand blender may be used after cooking to make a smooth mixture.) Add more water if necessary during cooking. Chill before using. Makes 3 - 5 dozen.

* Use solid margarine; see page 4 for explanation.
** If figs are very dry, soak in water overnight before cooking.

Cherry Surprises

This recipe, popular in the '40s and '50s, has never lost its appeal.

1 cup	butter or margarine*, softened	250	mL
1/4 cup	icing sugar	60	mL
1 tsp.	vanilla	5	mL
2 cups	all-purpose flour	500	mL
1/2 tsp.	salt	2	mL
1 cup	finely-chopped nuts	250	mL
48	maraschino cherries, well drained	48	
	Icing sugar		

Preheat oven to 325°F (160°C).

In a medium bowl, cream butter, the 1/4 cup (60 mL) icing sugar and vanilla. Stir in about three-quarters of the flour, along with the salt and nuts. Gradually mix in remaining flour until dough is workable but not sticky.

Bake a test cookie; see page 6 for directions.

Using about 2 teaspoons (10 mL) dough, completely encase each cherry. Place on ungreased cookie sheet. Bake for 30 minutes or until lightly browned. Shake hot cookies in a bag with icing sugar. Transfer to racks to cool.

Makes about 4 dozen.

* Use solid margarine; see page 4 for explanation.

Date Ribbons

We discovered this recipe in a 1967 cookbook.
Don't let the simplicity of it mislead you; the end product is
attractive, unusual and delicious.
Requires chilling.

30 graham wafers
Date Filling
Vanilla or Chocolate Icing

To make each stack, sandwich 5 graham wafers with date filling. Cover sides, then top of each stack with Vanilla or Chocolate Icing. Chill for at least 3 hours.

To serve, cut each stack into 1/2-inch slices or cut from corner to corner, making each stack into 4 triangles.

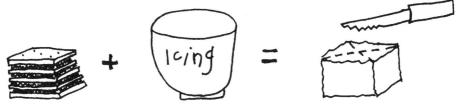

Date Filling

1 cup	chopped dates	250 mL
1/2 cup	water	125 mL
1/4 cup	granulated sugar	50 mL

In a heavy saucepan over medium heat, combine ingredients and bring to a boil. Reduce heat to low. Cook until smooth and thick, stirring often.

Vanilla or Chocolate Icing

1/4 cup	butter or margarine, softened	50 mL
1 1/2 cups	icing sugar	375 mL
3 tbsp.	cocoa (optional)	50 mL
1 tbsp.	milk	15 mL
1 tsp.	vanilla	5 mL

In a small bowl, combine ingredients until smooth.

Makes 2 - 4 dozen.

Carrot Cookies

A colourful and tasty family favourite.
Make cookies smaller for an attractive tea tray addition.

	Orange Frosting	
3/4 cup	shortening, softened	175 mL
3/4 cup	granulated sugar	175 mL
1	egg	1
1 tsp.	vanilla	5 mL
2 tsp.	baking powder	10 mL
1/2 tsp.	salt	2 mL
1 3/4 cups	all-purpose flour	425 mL
1 cup	grated carrot	250 mL
1 cup	chopped nuts	250 mL

Prepare Orange Frosting. Cover until ready to use.

Preheat oven to 375°F (190°C).

In a large bowl, cream shortening and sugar. Beat in egg, vanilla, baking powder and salt. Stir in flour. Mix in carrots and nuts.

Bake a test cookie; see page 6 for directions.

Drop from a teaspoon onto greased cookie sheet. Bake for 15 minutes or until delicately browned. Transfer to racks and gently frost cookies while hot.

	Orange Frosting	
1 1/2 cups	icing sugar	375 mL
2 tbsp	orange juice	30 mL
2 tbsp.	butter or margarine, softened	30 mL
	Grated peel of one orange	

In a small bowl, combine all ingredients until smooth.

Makes 3 - 4 dozen.

Snappy Turtles

A treat for kids and kids at heart. If serving to children,
be sure they are old enough to safely handle nuts.

1/2 cup	butter, softened	125	mL
1/2 cup	brown sugar	125	mL
1	egg, separated	1	
3/4 tsp.	vanilla	3	mL
1 1/2 cups	all-purpose flour	375	mL
1/4 tsp.	baking soda	1	mL
1/4 tsp.	salt	1	mL
3	packages (100 g) pecan halves	3	
3	squares semi-sweet chocolate, melted	3	

Preheat oven to 350°F (180°C).

In a medium bowl, cream butter and sugar. Beat in egg yolk and vanilla. Thoroughly blend in flour, baking soda and salt. Dough will be soft.

Bake a test cookie; dough should spread enough to resemble a turtle shell. See page 6 for directions.

Arrange pecans in groups of five on greased cookie sheet to resemble head and legs of turtle. Using 1 teaspoon (5 mL) of dough, shape balls, dip in egg white, and press lightly onto nuts. Bake for 12 minutes or until lightly browned on edges. Loosen any cookies that are sticking to the cookie sheet. Top with melted chocolate while warm. Transfer to racks to cool.

Makes 2 - 3 dozen.

Cracked-Top Sugar Cookies

This old-time cookie has a lovely "sugar cookie" flavour, and no rolling or cutting is required. Add cherries or raisins for a flavourful variation.

1 cup	butter or margarine*, softened	250	mL
1/2 cup	granulated sugar	125	mL
1/2 cup	brown sugar	125	mL
1	egg	1	
2 tsp.	cream of tartar	10	mL
1 tsp.	baking soda	5	mL
1/4 tsp.	salt	1	mL
2 1/4 cups	all-purpose flour	550	mL
	Granulated sugar		

Preheat oven to 350°F (180°C).

In a medium bowl, cream butter and sugars. Beat in egg, cream of tartar, baking soda and salt. Stir in flour.

Bake a test cookie; see page 6 for directions.

Shape into 1-inch (2.5 cm) balls. Shake a few at a time in a bag with granulated sugar. Place on ungreased cookie sheet. Flatten with a fork. Bake for 10 minutes, or until bottoms are golden brown. Transfer to racks to cool.

Makes about 4 dozen.

Variation:

For a tasty, quite different kind of cookie, add 1 cup (250 mL) chopped candied cherries (particularly nice at Christmas time) or 1 cup raisins (good all year round). Omit shaking in the granulated sugar.

* Use solid margarine; see page 4 for explanation.

Do not use warm cookie sheets.

Always place dough on a cold cookie sheet. If it is warm, the fat in the dough melts and the cookies will spread too much.

Date-Filled Sandwich Cookies

A unique oatmeal cookie — wonderful filled or unfilled.

2 cups	rolled oats	500	mL
2 cups	all-purpose flour	500	mL
1 cup	granulated sugar	250	mL
1 tsp.	baking soda	5	mL
1/2 tsp.	salt	2	mL
1 cup	butter or margarine*	250	mL
1/2 cup	milk	125	mL
2 tsp.	vinegar	10	mL
1 tsp.	vanilla (optional)	5	mL
	Date Filling (p. 77)		

In a large bowl, combine oats, flour, sugar, baking soda and salt. Using a pastry blender or two knives, cut in butter until mixture resembles fine crumbs.

Stir vinegar and vanilla into milk. Combine with dry ingredients, holding back a little of the liquid. Dough should be moist enough to hold together and roll without cracking. Add remainder of milk mixture if needed. Cover dough and let stand 30 minutes. This makes the dough easier to handle. (Dough can also be wrapped and kept refrigerated at this point. When ready to use, let stand at room temperature about 30 minutes before rolling.)

Preheat oven to 375°F (190°C).

On a lightly-floured surface, roll dough to 1/8 inch (3 mm) thickness. Cut with sharp round cookie cutter. Place on ungreased cookie sheet. Bake for 8 minutes or until browned on bottom and just beginning to brown on edges. Immediately transfer to racks to cool. Put about 1/2 tablespoon (7 mL) date filling between two cookies. The filled cookies soften upon standing; if crisp cookies are preferred, fill just before serving.

Makes 3 - 4 dozen filled cookies.

* Use solid margarine; see page 4 for explanation.

"Small Cakes"

Cookbooks written prior to about 1930 do not appear to have a cookie section. Cookie recipes were in a category called small cakes.

Some Things Change

Since beginning work on this book, we have looked at many cookbooks, including some early ones. We were particularly enchanted with *Dods' Cookery,* published in 1837 in London, England. Mistress Margaret Dods wasted neither words nor space. General instructions were given at the beginning of each section, followed by recipes which were short and to the point. Here are two, reproduced in the original type size.

Cinnamon Cakes Whisk six eggs with a glass of rose-water; add a pound of sifted sugar and a quarter-ounce of ground cinnamon, and stamp it into small cakes. Bake them on paper. They may be iced, or have sifted sugar strewed over them.

Kent Drop-Cakes A pound of flour, a half-pound of butter, the same of sifted sugar and currants. Make this into a paste with two eggs, two spoonfuls of orange-flower water, a glass of brandy, and one of sweet wine. Mix up quickly, and drop the batter through a biscuit-funnel on floured tins, and bake for five or six minutes.

...and some things never do!

We were delighted to note that the philosophy and goals expressed by Mistress Dods were very close to those we had established for this cookie book. Here they are — our thoughts in 1837 language.

"Almost every receipt has been revised, both with the view of increasing the sum of information, and of rendering the direction as plain as possible — as every one is aware that culinary directions, like those of surgeons and apothecaries, are liable to be strangely misunderstood.

"It may be thought that some of the more common processes of the kitchen are too elaborately described in this work, and also that some of the plain receipts are too minute in their detail. But every Manual of Art is presumed to be written for the benefit of the uninstructed; and to the young cook and housekeeper it is impossible to magnify too much the importance of Culinary Science and domestic management, or too carefully to obviate their difficulties.

"They (the readers) may at all times walk confidently by the letter of our instructions; but they will fall short of the full advantage, unless, excercising their own understandings, and applying their own increasing experience, they learn to apprehend the spirit in the letter and to act in all circumstances accordingly."

In reading this, we were reminded once again that cooking is as much an art as it is a science. We trust that our detailed recipes and numerous tips will provide the framework, and that users of our book will apply creativity to their cookie-making experiences. Above all, we wish for everyone a sense of enjoyment and success.

Food for the Gods

A good-tasting bar that uses few ingredients.

3/4 cup	graham wafer crumbs	175	mL
1 cup	brown sugar	250	mL
1 cup	chopped nuts	250	mL
1 cup	cut-up dates	250	mL
2	eggs, beaten	2	

Preheat oven to 350°F (180°C).

In a medium bowl, combine crumbs, sugar, nuts and dates. Thoroughly mix in eggs. Press into greased 8-inch (20 cm) square pan. Bake for 25 minutes or until golden brown.

Makes about 2 dozen.

Variation:

Substitute cut-up candied cherries for up to half the dates.

Rickety Uncles

This recipe has been passed along through several generations. You may know it as Scotch Teas, Oatmeal Tea Squares, or Butterscotch Oat Thins.

1/2 cup	butter or margarine*	125	mL
1 cup	brown sugar	250	mL
2 cups	rolled oats	500	mL
1 tsp.	baking powder	5	mL
1/2 tsp.	salt	2	mL

Preheat oven to 300°F (150°C).

In a large saucepan over medium heat, melt butter. Stir in sugar. Remove from heat. Stir in remaining ingredients. Press into ungreased 8-inch (20 cm) square pan. Bake for 20 minutes or until lightly browned.

Makes about 2 dozen.

Variations:

Crispy Uncles: Reduce rolled oats to 1 1/2 cups (375 mL) and add 1 cup (250 mL) crispy rice cereal. Bake in 9-inch (22 cm) square pan.

For a special occasion, put a dab of white butter icing on each piece and top with a bit of candied cherry.

* Use solid margarine; see page 4 for explanation.

Butterscotch Bars

Quick and easy.
Mix right in the saucepan used to melt the butter.

1/4 cup	butter	60	mL
1 cup	brown sugar	250	mL
1	egg	1	
1 1/2 tsp.	vanilla	7	mL
2/3 cup	all-purpose flour	150	mL
1 tsp.	baking powder	5	mL
1/4 tsp.	salt	1	mL
1/4 cup	chopped nuts	50	mL

Preheat oven to 350°F (180°C).

In a medium saucepan, melt butter. Remove from heat and blend in sugar. Thoroughly stir in egg and vanilla. Blend in flour, baking powder and salt. Mix in nuts. Spread in greased 8-inch (20 cm) square baking pan. Bake for 25 minutes or until set in centre but still soft. Cool and cut into bars.

Makes about 2 dozen.

Variation:

Stir in 1/2 cup (125 mL) chopped dates along with the nuts.

 It is not necessary to sift flour when making cookies or bars.

Chinese Chews

Another old favourite recycled.

2	eggs	2	
1 cup	brown sugar	250	mL
1 cup	chopped walnuts	250	mL
1 cup	cut-up dates	250	mL
1 tsp.	vanilla	5	mL
1 tsp.	baking powder	5	mL
2/3 cup	all-purpose flour	150	mL
	Granulated sugar		

Preheat oven to 350°F (180°C).

In a medium bowl, thoroughly beat eggs and sugar. Stir in walnuts, dates, vanilla and baking powder. Blend in flour. Spread in greased 9 x 13-inch (22 x 34 cm) baking pan.

Bake for 20 minutes or until browned around edges. Cut, while hot, into small rectangles and shape with hands into tiny rolls. Roll in sugar. Cool.

Makes 3 - 4 dozen.

Date Fingers

This simple, easy recipe was a favourite
with everyone who tasted it.

1 tbsp.	butter or margarine*, softened	15	mL
3 tbsp.	icing sugar	50	mL
2	eggs	2	
1 tsp.	vanilla	5	mL
1 tsp.	baking powder	5	mL
1/8 tsp.	salt	0.5	mL
3 tbsp.	all-purpose flour	50	mL
1/2 cup	finely chopped walnuts	125	mL
1 cup	finely chopped dates	250	mL
	Icing sugar		

Preheat oven to 325°F (160°C).

In a medium bowl, cream butter and sugar until light and fluffy. Beat in eggs, vanilla, baking powder and salt. Blend in flour. Stir in nuts and dates. Spread evenly in greased 8-inch (20 cm) square baking pan. Bake for 25 minutes or until browned. While hot, cut into finger lengths and sprinkle with icing sugar.

Makes about 2 - 3 dozen.

* Use solid margarine; see page 4 for explanation.

Raisin Marguerites

These cookies are high in fibre. The recipe, from a 1932 cookbook, is tasty and interesting. Opinions were divided about the soda cracker base — people either loved or hated it. We suggest you try making some both ways to reach your own conclusion.

1 cup	walnuts	250 mL
1 cup	raisins	250 mL
1 cup	coconut	250 mL
1 cup	currants	250 mL
2	egg whites	2
1/2 cup	granulated sugar	125 mL
	Soda crackers (optional)	

Preheat oven to 250°F (120°C).

Put walnuts, raisins, coconut and currants through food chopper. Or using a food processor, chop nuts for 20 seconds. Add raisins, coconut and currants; process with on/off motion for another 40 seconds or until minced.

In a medium bowl, beat egg whites until soft peaks form. Gradually beat in sugar, 2 tablespoons (25 mL) at a time. Continue beating until stiff and glossy. Fold in minced nuts and fruit.

Drop mixture from a teaspoon onto a cookie sheet lined with cooking parchment or brown paper. Or spread mixture on soda crackers, taking care to cover entire cracker; these may be baked on an ungreased cookie sheet. Bake for 45 minutes or until nicely browned. Transfer to racks to cool.

Makes 2 - 3 dozen.

Beating Egg Whites

When beating egg whites, it is important that no fat is present. This means separating the egg carefully so no yolk gets into the white, and using beaters and bowls that are free of any fat. Glass or metal bowls are recommended; plastic often retains a film that interferes with beating.

Pecan Puffs

Attractive, rich, excellent flavour.

1 cup	butter, softened (do not use margarine)	250	mL
1/4 cup	berry sugar	60	mL
1/2 tsp.	salt	2	mL
1 3/4 cups	all-purpose flour	425	mL
2 tbsp.	milk	30	mL
2 tsp.	vanilla	10	mL
2 cups	chopped pecans	500	mL
	Berry sugar*		

Preheat oven to 325°F (160°C).

In a medium bowl, cream butter thoroughly. Stir in sugar and salt. Mix in flour. Thoroughly blend in milk and vanilla, then nuts. Dough should be soft but not sticky. If it is difficult to handle, chill for 15 minutes.

Roll into 1-inch (2.5 cm) balls. Place on ungreased cookie sheet. Bake for 18 minutes or until barely browned. Roll warm cookies in berry sugar and place on racks to cool.

Makes about 4 dozen.

Berry sugar

Berry sugar is white sugar that is very finely granulated but not quite powdered. It can be purchased in that form, but is easily made at home by whirling granulated sugar briefly in a blender or food processor. Measure the required amount of berry sugar after blending.

Porcupines

One of our home economists, who is a grandmother herself,
said these took her back to her grandmother's kitchen.
Finicky to make, but unique and wonderful.

2	eggs	2
1 cup	brown sugar	250 mL
1 cup	chopped walnuts	250 mL
1 cup	chopped dates	250 mL
2 cups	shredded or flaked coconut	500 mL

Preheat oven to 325°F (160°C).

In a medium bowl, beat eggs and sugar. Thoroughly mix in nuts and dates.

Drop batter from a tablespoon into dish of coconut, about 4 at a time. Sprinkle coconut over each mound. Roll and press into oblong shape, coating it with coconut. Place on well-greased cookie sheet. Bake for 15 minutes or until delicately browned. Leave on pan for 5 minutes, then transfer to racks to finish cooling. Store in airtight container.

Makes 3 - 4 dozen.

These really *don't* contain any flour!

Coconut Macaroons

This truly is an "oldie but goodie". It appeared in many of the old cookbooks, and it's as nice an addition to a cookie tray today as it was decades ago.

4	egg whites	4
1/2 tsp.	cream of tartar	2 mL
1/4 tsp.	salt	1 mL
1 tsp.	vanilla	5 mL
1 cup	granulated sugar	250 mL
2 cups	coconut	500 mL

Preheat oven to 300°F (150°C).

In a deep medium bowl, beat egg whites, cream of tartar, salt and vanilla until soft peaks form. Gradually add sugar, 2 tablespoons (25 mL) at a time, beating well after each addition. Continue beating until stiff and glossy. Fold in coconut.

Drop mixture from a teaspoon onto greased cookie sheet. Bake 20 minutes or until lightly browned. Allow to cool 5 minutes on cookie sheets, then transfer to racks to cool.

Makes about 7 dozen.

Variations:

Date Walnut Macaroons: Instead of coconut, fold in 1 1/2 cup (375 mL) finely chopped dates and 3/4 cup (175 mL) chopped walnuts.

Cherry Almond Macaroons: Substitute 1/2 teaspoon (2 mL) almond extract for the vanilla. Instead of coconut, fold in 1 cup (250 mL) cut-up candied cherries and 1/2 cup (125 mL) chopped almonds.

Fruity Macaroons: Instead of coconut, fold in 1/2 cup (125 mL) chopped figs, 1/2 cup (125 mL) raisins, and 1 cup (250 mL) chopped unsalted roasted peanuts.

Bird's Nests

A cookie whose origin goes way back,
these are also known as Thimble or Thumbprint Cookies.

1/2 cup	butter or margarine*, softened	125 mL
1/4 cup	granulated sugar	60 mL
1	egg, separated	1
1/2 tsp.	vanilla or almond flavouring	2 mL
1 cup	all-purpose flour	250 mL
3/4 cup	finely chopped walnuts or almonds	175 mL
	Jam or jelly	

Preheat oven to 350°F (180°C).

In a medium bowl, cream butter. Beat in sugar gradually, then beat in egg yolk and flavouring. Stir in flour.

Bake a test cookie; see page 6 for directions.

Roll dough into 3/4-inch (2 cm) balls. Dip into unbeaten egg white, then in the nuts. Place on greased cookie sheet and make an indentation in the centre with your thumb or finger.

Bake for 5 minutes, remove from oven, and indent cookies again, working quickly so they do not cool off. If you find them too hot, use a thimble. Continue baking for another 5 minutes or until golden on bottom. Transfer to racks to cool. Fill indentations with jam while cookies are hot, or store them unfilled and add jam just before serving.

Makes about 3 dozen.

* Use solid margarine; see page 4 for explanation.

Power-Packed Cookies

The bars and cookies in this section are high in energy, fibre and nutrients. The rolled oats, wheat germ, nuts, sunflower seeds and sesame seeds used in many of the recipes provide significant amounts of B-vitamins. Some of the recipes call for skim milk powder, which boosts the protein content. A number of the recipes are sugar-reduced. You may wish to experiment with reducing the sugar further in these or any of the recipes. Two of the recipes are sugar free.

We suggest that many of the recipes in this section make good breakfast foods for people on the run. Add a glass of milk and a fruit rich in vitamin C (oranges, grapefruit, strawberries, canteloupe, kiwi) and you have a breakfast of quality.

Dropped

Shaped

Refrigerator

Bar

Power-Packed Cookies

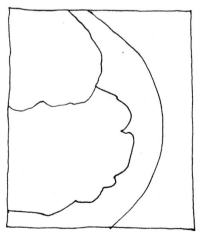

Peanut Butter Biggies p. 163

Peanut Butter Biggies

Moist and flavourful.

1 cup	butter or margarine*, softened	250 mL
1 cup	chunky or smooth peanut butter	250 mL
1 1/2 cups	brown sugar	375 mL
2	eggs	2
2 tsp.	baking soda	10 mL
1/2 tsp.	salt	2 mL
1/2 tsp.	ground cinnamon	2 mL
1 3/4 cups	whole wheat flour	425 mL
2/3 cup	rolled oats	150 mL
1/3 cup	wheat germ	75 mL
1/4 cup	powdered milk	50 mL
1 1/2 cups	finely chopped peeled apple	375 mL

Preheat oven to 350°F (180°C).

In a large bowl, cream butter and peanut butter. Beat in sugar, eggs, baking soda, salt and cinnamon. Stir in flour, then rolled oats, wheat germ and powdered milk. Mix in apple.

Bake a test cookie; see page 6 for directions.

Shape into 1 1/2-inch (4 cm) balls. Place on ungreased cookie sheet. Flatten with a fork. Bake for 14 minutes or until lightly browned and firm to the touch. Transfer to racks to cool.

Makes 3 - 4 dozen.

* Use solid margarine; see page 4 for explanation.

Children's Cottage—love in action

From a client: "Thank you all very much for your loving care of my son. This note is hopelessly inadequate as an expression of my gratitude. I feel that you really saved our lives."

Sunnies

A crisp, delicate cookie with
the zesty taste of orange and lemon.

1/2 cup	butter or margarine*, softened	125	mL
3/4 cup	brown sugar	175	mL
1/2 cup	rolled oats	125	mL
1/4 cup	wheat germ	50	mL
1/4 cup	powdered milk	50	mL
2/3 cup	roasted salted sunflower seeds	150	mL
1/3 cup	finely chopped almonds, pecans or walnuts	75	mL
1 tsp.	vanilla	5	mL
2 tsp.	grated orange peel	10	mL
1/2 tsp.	grated lemon peel	2	mL
1 tbsp.	milk	15	mL

Preheat oven to 350°F (180°C).

In a medium bowl, cream butter and sugar until light and fluffy. Stir in rolled oats, wheat germ, powdered milk, sunflower seeds, nuts, vanilla and peels. Add milk, blending well.

Bake a test cookie; it should be thin and lacy. See page 6 for directions.

Drop batter from a teaspoon, 2 inches (5 cm) apart, onto cookie sheet that is either well greased, made with a non-stick surface, or lined with cooking parchment. Bake for 8 minutes or until lightly browned. Cool on sheet 2 - 3 minutes, then loosen with wide spatula. If cookies break apart, gently press back together. Cool on sheet 2 minutes longer, then transfer to racks to cool completely. If cookies stick to the cookie sheet, put them back in oven briefly to soften. Store in airtight container to retain crispness.

Makes 2 - 3 dozen.

* Use solid margarine; see page 4 for explanation.

Power Cookies

A cookie with staying power!

1/2 cup	peanut butter	125	mL
1/2 cup	honey	125	mL
1 cup	brown sugar	250	mL
1/2 cup	vegetable oil	125	mL
2	eggs	2	
1/2 tsp.	vanilla	2	mL
1 cup	whole wheat flour	250	mL
1 tsp.	baking soda	5	mL
1 tsp.	salt	5	mL
3 cups	rolled oats	750	mL
1 cup	coconut	250	mL
1/2 cup	bran	125	mL
1/4 cup	wheat germ	50	mL
1/2 cup	oat bran	125	mL
1 cup	raisins	250	mL
1/2 cup	chopped peanuts	125	mL

Preheat oven to 375°F (190°C).

In a large bowl, cream peanut butter and honey. Beat in sugar, oil, eggs and vanilla. Stir in flour, baking soda and salt. Add remaining ingredients and stir well.

Bake a test cookie; see page 6 for directions.

With slightly-dampened hands, shape dough into walnut-sized balls. Place on greased cookie sheet and flatten with fingers. Bake for 10 minutes or until browned on the bottom. Transfer to racks to cool.

Makes about 4 dozen.

Surprise Cookies

"Excellent flavour — definitely a taster's choice" according to
the home economist who tested this unusual recipe.

1/2 cup	butter or margarine*, softened	125 mL
1/4 cup	granulated sugar	50 mL
1	egg	1
1 cup	all-purpose flour	250 mL
1/2 tsp.	baking powder	2 mL
1 cup	grated medium cheddar cheese	250 mL
2 cups	bran flakes	500 mL
3/4 cup	raisins, nuts, and/or seeds	175 mL

Preheat oven to 350°F (180°C).

In a large bowl, cream butter and sugar. Beat in egg. Stir in flour and baking powder. Mix in remaining ingredients.

Bake a test cookie; see page 6 for directions.

Drop batter from a teaspoon onto greased cookie sheet. Bake 12 minutes or until golden brown. Transfer to racks to cool.

Makes about 3 dozen.

* Use solid margarine; see page 4 for explanation.

Many of the recipes in this section make good breakfast foods for people on the run. Add a glass of milk and fruit rich in vitamin C, such as oranges, grapefruit, strawberries, canteloupe or kiwi. Together they make a quality breakfast.

Bran Raisin Cookies

High fiber, tasty and easy to make.

1 cup	butter or margarine*, softened	250	mL
1 cup	brown sugar	250	mL
2	eggs	2	
1 1/2 tsp	vanilla	7	mL
1 1/2 cups	all-purpose or whole-wheat flour	375	mL
1 tsp.	baking soda	5	mL
1 tsp.	ground cinnamon	5	mL
1 1/2 cups	bran flakes	375	mL
1 cup	raisins	250	mL

Preheat oven to 375°F (190°C).

In a large bowl, cream butter and sugar. Beat in eggs and vanilla. Thoroughly stir in flour, baking soda and cinnamon. Mix in bran flakes and raisins.

Bake a test cookie; see page 6 for directions.

Drop batter from a teaspoon 2 inches (5 cm) apart onto ungreased cookie sheet. Bake for 12 minutes or until golden brown. Transfer to racks to cool.

Makes about 3 dozen.

* Use solid margarine; see page 4 for explanation.

Chewy Ginger Cookies

A *good* lunchbox cookie.

1/2 cup	vegetable oil	125 mL
1/2 cup	molasses	125 mL
1/2 cup	honey	125 mL
1	egg	1
2 1/2 cups	whole wheat flour	625 mL
1/2 cup	powdered milk	125 mL
1/4 cup	wheat germ	50 mL
2 tsp.	baking soda	10 mL
1 tsp.	ground cinnamon	5 mL
3 tbsp.	freshly grated ginger root*	50 mL

Preheat oven to 350°F (180°C)

In a medium bowl, beat oil, molasses, honey and egg.

In a large bowl, combine remaining ingredients. Add the molasses mixture. Combine thoroughly but do not overmix; batter will be quite thick.

Bake a test cookie; see page 6 for directions.

Drop batter from a teaspoon onto greased cookie sheet. Bake for 10 minutes or until set. Transfer to racks to cool.

Makes about 4 dozen.

* 1 tablespoon (15 mL) or more ground dry ginger may be used instead.

Measuring sticky liquids

Honey, molasses and corn syrup slide out of the measuring cup very easily if it is lightly oiled before measuring. The no-fuss way of oiling a measuring cup is to pour vegetable oil into the clean cup, then pour it back into the bottle. The oil that clings to the cup is just the right amount to do the job. When a recipe calls for oil, as does the one above, measure the oil first and use the same cup for honey and molasses.

Children's Cottage Cookie Cook Book

Sugarless Date Cookies

These cookies are not sweet. The only sweetening comes from the dates, so your taste buds may need adjusting.
Dough requires chilling.

2/3 cup	all-purpose flour	150 mL
1/2 cup	whole wheat flour	125 mL
1/2 cup	wheat germ	125 mL
1/2 cup	powdered milk	125 mL
1 tsp.	baking powder	5 mL
1/4 tsp.	salt	1 mL
1/2 cup	butter or margarine*, softened	125 mL
2	eggs	2
1 1/2 tsp.	vanilla	7 mL
1 tsp.	grated orange or lemon rind	5 mL
1 2/3 cups	chopped dates	400 mL
1 cup	unsweetened shredded coconut	250 mL
1/2 cup	chopped walnuts	125 mL
1/2 cup	chopped unsalted sunflower seeds	125 mL

In a medium bowl, combine flours, wheat germ, powdered milk, baking powder and salt.

In another bowl, cream butter, eggs and vanilla until light and fluffy. Mix in grated rind. Gradually stir in flour mixture. Mix in dates, coconut, nuts and seeds. Form dough into two rolls 1 1/2-inches (4 cm) in diameter. Wrap in plastic and refrigerate for several hours or overnight.

Preheat oven to 350°F (180°C).

With a thin sharp knife, cut 3/8-inch (9 mm) slices. Place on lightly greased cookie sheet. If slices fall apart, press back into shape. Bake for 12 minutes or until golden and firm to touch. Transfer to racks to cool.

Makes 3 - 4 dozen.

* Use solid margarine; see page 4 for explanation.

Sugarless Banana Cookies

The banana provides delicate flavour and a little sweetening in these nutritious cookies.

1 1/2 cups	rolled oats	375	mL
1/2 cup	whole wheat or all-purpose flour	125	mL
1/3 cup	sunflower seeds	75	mL
1/4 cup	toasted wheat germ	50	mL
1 1/2 tsp.	baking powder	7	mL
1/2 tsp.	salt	2	mL
1 1/2 tsp.	cinnamon	7	mL
1	egg, slightly beaten	1	
1 cup	mashed banana	250	mL
1/3 cup	oil	75	mL
2 tbsp.	milk	30	mL

Preheat oven to 350°F (180°C).

In a medium bowl, combine rolled oats, flour, sunflower seeds, wheat germ, baking powder, salt and cinnamon.

In another bowl, combine egg, banana, oil and milk. Add to dry ingredients, stirring until well blended.

Bake a test cookie; see page 6 for directions.

Drop dough from a teaspoon onto well-greased cookie sheet. Press with fork dipped lightly in flour. Bake for 12 minutes or until golden on bottom. These cookies change colour very little on top during baking. Transfer to racks to cool.

Makes 2 - 3 dozen.

Fruit Bars

High in energy, nutrients and flavour.

3 cups	whole wheat flour	750	mL
3/4 cup	all-purpose flour	175	mL
1/2 cup	wheat germ	125	mL
1 cup	brown sugar	250	mL
1 cup	powdered milk	250	mL
2 tsp.	baking powder	10	mL
1 tsp.	salt	5	mL
2 tsp.	ground cinnamon	10	mL
2	eggs	2	
2 cups	apple juice	500	mL
3/4 cup	vegetable oil	175	mL
1/2 cup	honey	125	mL
1/2 cup	dark corn syrup	125	mL
2 tsp.	grated orange peel	10	mL
2 tsp.	vanilla	10	mL
2 cups	raisins	500	mL
1	package (250 g) dried apricots, cut up	1	
1 cup	salted roasted sunflower seeds	250	mL

Preheat oven to 350°F (180°C).

In a large bowl, combine flours, wheat germ, sugar, powdered milk, baking powder, salt and cinnamon.

In another large bowl, beat eggs. Beat in apple juice, oil, honey, corn syrup, orange peel and vanilla. Add dry ingredients, stirring just until moistened. Mix in fruit and seeds. Spread in greased 10 x 15-inch (25 x 40 cm) jelly roll pan. Bake for 45 minutes or until a toothpick inserted in centre comes out clean.

Makes 3 - 4 dozen.

Cutting bars

Cool bars thoroughly before cutting, unless otherwise specified in the recipe.

Seed Bars

Good for lunches; easy to make.

2 cups	rolled oats	500	mL
3/4 cup	flaked coconut	175	mL
1/4 cup	toasted sunflower seeds	50	mL
1/4 cup	sesame seeds	50	mL
1/2 tsp.	salt	2	mL
1/3 cup	peanut butter	75	mL
1/2 cup	liquid honey	125	mL
1/4 cup	vegetable oil	50	mL

Preheat oven to 300°F (150°C).

In a medium bowl, combine rolled oats, coconut, sunflower seeds, sesame seeds and salt.

In another bowl, combine peanut butter, honey and oil. Pour over dry ingredients. Mix thoroughly. Press into greased 9 x 13-inch (22 x 34 cm) baking pan. Bake for 25 minutes or until lightly browned. Store in an airtight container.

Makes about 2 dozen.

Apricot Almond Bars

One of these isn't enough!

1/2 cup	butter or margarine*	125	mL
1/2 cup	liquid honey	125	mL
1 cup	diced dried apricots	250	mL
2 cups	granola cereal	500	mL
3/4 cup	sesame seeds, divided	175	mL
1/2 cup	sunflower seeds	125	mL
1/2 cup	skim milk powder	125	mL
1/2 cup	chopped almonds	125	mL
1/2 cup	all-purpose or whole wheat flour	125	mL
2	eggs, beaten	2	
1 tsp.	vanilla	5	mL
1/2 tsp.	almond extract	2	mL

Preheat oven to 325°F (160°C).

In a small saucepan over medium heat, melt butter. Stir in honey until dissolved. Remove from heat and stir in apricots. Cool to room temperature.

In a large bowl, combine granola, 1/2 cup (125 mL) of the sesame seeds, sunflower seeds, skim milk powder, almonds and flour.

To cooled butter mixture, add eggs, vanilla, and almond extract; stir well. Add to granola mixture and combine thoroughly. Spread in greased 9 x 13-inch (22 x 34 cm) baking pan. Sprinkle with remaining 1/4 cup (50 mL) sesame seeds. Bake for 25 minutes or until browned around the edges.

Makes about 2 dozen.

* Use solid margarine; see page 4 for explanation.

Dark or light pans— it makes a difference.

Light, shiny cookie sheets and baking pans result in lightly-browned bars and cookies. Dark pans absorb heat and may result in over-browned bottoms.

Wonder Bars

Wonder-ful!

1 cup	peanut butter	250	mL
1/3 cup	butter or margarine*, softened	75	mL
1/2 cup	corn syrup	125	mL
1/2 cup	brown sugar	125	mL
1 tsp.	vanilla	5	mL
3 cups	rolled oats	750	mL
1/2 cup	coconut	125	mL
1/2 cup	sunflower seeds	125	mL
1/2 cup	raisins	125	mL
1/3 cup	wheat germ	75	mL
3/4 cup	chocolate chips (optional)	175	mL

Preheat oven to 350°F (180°C).

In a large bowl, cream peanut butter and butter. Beat in corn syrup, brown sugar and vanilla. Stir in oats, coconut, sunflower seeds, raisins and wheat germ; mix well. Stir in chocolate chips. Pat into 9 x 13-inch (22 x 34 cm) baking pan. Bake for 20 minutes or until light golden brown.

Makes about 2 dozen.

* Use solid margarine; see page 4 for explanation.

The rolled oats, wheat germ, nuts, sunflower seeds and sesame seeds used in many of the recipes in this section provided significant amounts of B vitamins.

Coconut Bars

Chewy; excellent flavour.

3 cups	rolled oats	750	mL
2 cups	coconut	500	mL
1 cup	chopped nuts (peanuts are good)	250	mL
1/2 cup	wheat germ	125	mL
1/2 cup	sesame seeds	125	mL
1/2 cup	sunflower seeds	125	mL
1 cup	raisins	250	mL
1/2 tsp.	salt	2	mL
3/4 cup	butter or margarine*, melted	175	mL
1/2 cup	liquid honey	125	mL
3	eggs	3	
1 tsp.	vanilla	5	mL

Preheat oven to 350°F (180°C).

In a large bowl, combine oats, coconut, nuts, wheat germ, sesame seeds, sunflower seeds, raisins and salt.

In another bowl, combine melted butter, honey, eggs and vanilla until well blended. Pour over dry ingredients and mix to combine. Press into 10 x 15-inch (25 x 40 cm) jelly roll pan. Bake for 20 minutes or until golden brown.

Makes about 3 dozen.

* Use solid margarine; see page 4 for explanation.

Toffee Bars

These bars are a great high-energy food for hikers.

2 cups	rolled oats	500	mL
1/2 cup	all-purpose or whole wheat flour	125	mL
1	package (100 g) slivered almonds	1	
3/4 cup	chopped roasted peanuts	175	mL
1/2 cup	coconut	125	mL
1/2 cup	raisins	125	mL
3/4 cup	butter or margarine*	175	mL
1 1/2 cups	brown sugar	375	mL
1/2 cup	milk	125	mL
1/2 tsp.	salt	2	mL
1 tsp.	vanilla	5	mL

Preheat oven to 350°F (180°C).

In a large bowl, combine rolled oats, flour, almonds, peanuts, coconut and raisins.

In a small saucepan over low heat, combine butter, sugar, milk and salt. Stir until butter melts and mixture is blended. Bring to a boil, and boil for 8 minutes. Stir in vanilla. Stir hot mixture into dry ingredients. Press into greased 9 x 13-inch (22 x 34 cm) baking pan. Bake for 20 minutes or until browned.

Makes about 2 dozen.

* Use solid margarine; see page 4 for explanation.

Fun for Kids
(and kids at ♡)

Time to Create!

Unbaked Treats

Fun For Kids
(and Kids at ♡)

Chocolate Chip Cookie Cottage p. 179

Chocolate Chip Cookie Cottage

This fun-to-make cottage is pictured at the beginning
of this section. The assembly instructions are explicit,
but decorating it allows plenty of room for your imagination.

3/4 cup	butter or margarine*, softened	175 mL
3/4 cup	shortening, softened	175 mL
1 cup	granulated sugar	250 mL
1 cup	brown sugar	250 mL
3	eggs	3
1 tsp.	vanilla	5 mL
3 1/2 cups	all-purpose flour	875 mL
1 1/2 tsp.	baking soda	7 mL
1 tsp.	salt	5 mL
1	package (300 g) chocolate chips	1
1 cup	chopped walnuts or pecans (optional)	250 mL
	Icing Cement	
	Candies for decorating	
	Sturdy board or tray	

Preheat oven to 375°F (190°C).

In a large bowl, cream butter, shortening and sugars until fluffy. Beat in eggs and vanilla. In a medium bowl, combine flour, baking soda and salt. Thoroughly stir into creamed mixture, one third at a time, to make a soft dough. Mix in chocolate chips and nuts.

Spread into two well-greased 10 x 15-inch (25 x 40 cm) jelly roll pans. This looks messy but ends up baking together in a solid piece. Bake for 20 minutes or until golden brown. Cool in pan for about 5 minutes, then cut house sections (see diagram). When completely cool, remove from pan carefully with a wide, sturdy spatula. Set on racks. When ready to assemble the cottage, prepare Icing Cement.

* Use solid margarine; see page 4 for explanation.

Icing Cement

6	egg whites	6
1/2 tsp.	cream of tartar	2 mL
8 cups	icing sugar	2 L

In a large bowl, beat egg whites and cream of tartar until foamy, white and doubled in volume. Sift the icing sugar into the whites, 1/2 cup (125 mL) at a time, beating thoroughly after each addition with an electric mixer. Continue beating until a stiff icing is formed (i.e. a knife drawn through mixture leaves a cleanly cut path).

Half fill a pastry bag fitted with a round decorating tip. Cover remaining icing with a dampened cloth and use within a few hours.

Makes 2 cottages, or 1 cottage on a chocolate chip base.

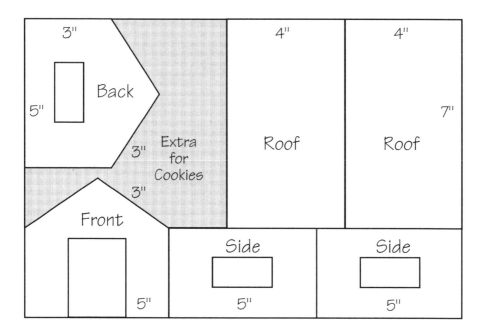

Guidelines for assembling the cottage:

1. Prepare a base by covering an 18 x 24-inch (45 x 60 cm) board with aluminum foil. If making only one cottage, the second half of the dough can be used for a base. Set on a sturdy piece of cardboard or tray for stability.

2. Using filled pastry bag, pipe a strip of frosting on the bottom of the back piece of the cottage. Place on board and hold until set. It helps at this stage to have a few extra hands or cans to lean the pieces against. Ice bottom and ends of the side pieces and put in place. Ice bottom of the front and put in place. Set door aside temporarily.

3. Trim windows and door frame with icing; decorate door with a tiny icing wreath. Secure door in place with icing.

4. Once foundation pieces are in place, attach the roof. Place icing all the way around the top edges of the house. Position roof pieces and hold gently for a few minutes until set.

5. Using a writing tip in pastry bag, decorate roof with shingles of icing. Using a heavy tip, decorate peak of roof with enough frosting to hold a chimney. Six or eight licorice lozenges arranged in circular fashion and topped with a small amount of icing (for snow or smoke) makes a good chimney.

6. Decorate roof with little icicles by drawing down a small amount of icing from edges of roof.

7. Use icing to make sidewalks. Smarties give a cobblestone effect, or why not a chocolate chip path?

8. More licorice lozenges (or other round coloured candies) are placed 1/2-inch apart to make a fence secured with frosting. Using a writing tip in the pastry bag, pipe fine icicles to link the lozenge "fence posts" together for a complete fence.

9. Ice cream cones make fine trees garnished with icing blobs and little candies. Fine coconut or icing sugar can be lightly sprinkled over the entire cottage for "snow".

Designer Gingerbread House

This interesting recipe gives instructions for designing your own gingerbread house. The contributor said she makes it every Christmas, then she and her family devour it on the Twelfth Night, candy and all. Nice custom!

1 1/2 cups	whipping cream	375	mL
1 tsp.	vanilla extract	5	mL
2 1/2 cups	firmly packed brown sugar	625	mL
2 tbsp.	baking soda	30	mL
1 tbsp.	ground ginger	15	mL
2 tsp.	ground cinnamon	10	mL
1 1/2 cups	light or dark molasses	375	mL
9 cups	all-purpose flour	2250	mL
	Icing Cement (page 180)		
	Cookies and candies for decorating		
	Sturdy board or tray		

In a large bowl, whip cream and vanilla until cream holds soft peaks.

In another large bowl, combine sugar, baking soda, ginger and cinnamon. Stir in molasses and cream. Gradually stir in flour, mixing well, until rolling consistency is achieved.

Determine what thickness your building slabs should be. For houses larger than 6 inches (15 cm) square, slabs should be rolled to 1/4 inch (6 mm). Smaller houses and decorative overlays can be 1/8 inch (3 mm) thick.

Grease and flour two rimless 12 x 15-inch (30 x 40 cm) cookie sheets. Locate two wooden strips the length of the cookie sheet and the thickness desired for the finished slabs.

On a lightly floured surface, roll out a portion of dough until it is flat but still thick enough to pick up easily without tearing. Use about 2 cups for a 1/8-inch/3 mm slab, or 4 cups for a 1/4-inch/6 mm slab. Transfer dough to prepared cookie sheet. Place wooden strips along opposite edges of pan. Finish rolling dough by supporting rolling pin on wooden strips. This will ensure slabs are evenly thick. If they are not, the thinner areas will bake darker in colour and will be more brittle.

Bake one or two pans of dough at a time, allowing about 1 hour at 300°F (150°C) for 1/8-inch (3 mm) slabs or 1 3/4 hours at 275°F (140°C) for 1/4-inch (6 mm) slabs. After the first 30 minutes of baking, remove pans from oven and place pattern pieces* close together on the dough. With a sharp knife, cut around pattern. Lift off pattern and scraps. Scraps can be baked later to eat. Return pans to oven, switching their positions, and continue baking until dough is fairly firm when pressed in centre. When done, carefully loosen pieces with spatula. Cool on cookie sheets for about 5 minutes or until firm. Transfer to racks to cool.

To assemble your structure, use Icing Cement to hold pieces together and to attach decorations. For ideas, refer to guidelines for assembling Chocolate Chip Cookie Cottage (page 181).

Makes 4 1/2 slabs 1/8-inch (3 mm) thick or 2 1/2 slabs 1/4-inch (6 mm) thick. Each slab is 10 x 15 inches (25 x 40 cm).

* Make these from your own design, cutting out of light cardboard. Test the design by taping the cardboard piece together; if you want to make changes, this is the time to do it. Size of pieces is limited to size of slab, which is 10 x 15 inches (25 x 40 cm).

Designer Cookies

- *Cookie cutters are not essential. Draw patterns on light cardboard or heavy paper, cut out, place on dough, and cut around edge with a sharp knife. Our recipe for Gingerbread Cookies gives you an example; of course, you can create any shape that strikes your fancy.*
- *For a birthday party activity, trace around each child's hand on a piece of paper. Cut out and use as your pattern. Each child can personalize his baked cookie hand by creating fingernails, rings and bracelets with icing and candies.*

Paintbrush Cookies

Good cookies and a fun activity for the little folks!
Dough requires chilling.

1/2 cup	shortening, softened	125 mL
1/3 cup	granulated sugar	75 mL
2/3 cup	liquid honey	150 mL
1	egg	1
1 tsp.	vanilla	5 mL
1 tsp.	baking soda	5 mL
1 tsp.	salt	5 mL
2 1/2 cups	all-purpose flour	625 mL
	Egg Yolk Paint	

In a medium bowl, cream shortening and sugar. Beat in honey, egg, vanilla, baking soda and salt. Stir in about three-quarters of the flour. Gradually add remaining flour, stopping when rolling consistency is achieved. Cover and chill 3 hours or overnight.

Preheat oven to 375°F (190°C).

On a lightly-floured surface, roll dough to a thickness of 1/4 inch (6 mm). Cut into desired shapes. Place on greased cookie sheet. Using a small clean paintbrush, paint designs with Egg Yolk Paint. Bake for 8 minutes or until lightly browned. Transfer to racks to cool.

Egg Yolk Paint

1	egg yolk	1
1/2 tsp.	water	2 mL
	Food colouring	

In a small dish, blend egg yolk and water. Divide among three or four small dishes. Stir a different food colour into each. If it thickens during use, stir in a few drops of water.

Makes about 3 dozen.

Safety tip

Although nuts are nutritious, they are also a potential choking hazard for young children. Avoid serving cookies with nuts to children until they are old enough to chew them slowly and thoroughly.

Christmas Mice

Don't limit these to kids — adults love them too!
Dough requires chilling for 1 hour.

**Peanut butter cookie dough (p 117)
or Halloween Lollipop dough (p 50)
Peanut halves
Green cherries or peel, slivered
Red licorice laces, cut into 3-inch (7 cm) lengths**

Prepare cookie dough, adding about 2 tablespoons (25 mL) more flour to make a slightly stiffer dough. Chill for 1 hour before shaping.

Preheat oven to 350°F (180°C).

Bake a test cookie; see page 6 for directions.

Shape dough into 1-inch balls. Taper each at one end, creating a teardrop shape. Press one side flat. Place on ungreased cookie sheet, pressing slightly to flatten bottom. Press in sides of ball to raise "backs" of mice, as dough spreads slightly during baking. Gently push in 2 peanut halves for ears, and 2 green pieces for eyes. With a toothpick, make a 1/2-inch (1 cm) deep hole at the tail end. Bake for 10 minutes or until firm. Transfer to racks, insert licorice tails, and cool completely.

Variation:

Birthday Mice: Shape as above. Before baking, use a toothpick to create a hole in the centre of the back to hold a birthday candle. Bake and finish as directed. Insert candles when cookies have partially cooled.

Fun with Marshmallows

Small children love creating and eating these easy-to-make treats.
> *Marshmallows, plain or coloured*
> *Milk*
> *Chocolate, graham wafer, or vanilla cookie crumbs*

Dip marshmallows on all sides in milk. Roll in cookie crumbs. Set on plate. Make as many as you want!

Uncookies

Small tots love these colourful "uncookies". In addition to being
fun party food, these cubes make an ideal snack. They are
not sticky, and can be carried in the car, or anywhere,
in a small container or plastic bag. This suggestion comes from a
young mother who tried it. Her 18-month-old daughter
loved it, and there were no sticky fingers!
Requires chilling.

1 cup	any flavour frozen fruit juice concentrate, thawed	250 mL
4	envelopes unflavoured gelatine	4
1 1/2 cups	boiling water	375 mL

In a medium bowl, combine juice concentrate and gelatine. Let stand for 5 minutes. Stir in boiling water, mixing until gelatine is dissolved. Pour into ungreased 8-inch (20 cm) square pan that has been rinsed with cold water. Chill for an hour or until firmly set.

To serve, cut into cubes, triangles or any desired shape. You can let your creativity (or your kids') take over with this recipe.

Makes enough for a few kids (for a while).

Variation:

Tri-colour Uncookie Ribbons Use three different juices, for example grape, orange and raspberry. Prepare first juice according to above instructions. Pour into ungreased 9 x 13-inch (22 x 34 cm) pan. Refrigerate until set firmly. Prepare second juice, pour over first juice layer and chill until set. Repeat with third juice. An attractive example of this recipe variation is to layer the orange juice between the grape and raspberry layers.

Ice Cream Cookie Sandwich

Spread peanut butter on an oatmeal cookie, then spread with softened ice cream and top with a second cookie. Prepare several at once to wrap and freeze for quick snacks.

Witches' Fingers

Halloween party fun for kids of all ages.

Crisp lady finger cookies*
Thin icing, tinted green**
Whole blanched almonds

Arrange lady fingers on wire racks. Set on cookie sheets. Spoon icing over cookies until evenly covered. Place an almond at one end of each cookie to make the witch's fingernail. Let stand until icing has hardened.

* The lady fingers must be a crisp type, not the traditional soft ones. The crisp variety are available in some delicatessens and speciality shops. Or instead, make our Biscotti recipe on page 38.
** Icing is made with icing sugar, water, a splash of vanilla and a drop of green food colouring.

Cut-Out Cookies

Making cut-out cookies is a fun activity for kids. There are several cut-out recipes in this book.

To create a rolled peanut butter cookie, add extra flour to the recipe on page 117 to make a dough which is stiff enough to roll.

You can decorate cookies before they are baked by sprinkling them with plain or coloured sugar, or by pressing into them lightly a few nuts, raisins, bits of citron, coconut, dates, figs, or candied fruit or peel. Or make a depression in the centre of each cookie and fill it with chocolate chips, jam or jelly, candied ginger, or candied orange or lemon peel.

Dirt Dessert

Dig right in!

1	package (450 g) white creme-filled chocolate cookies	1
1/4 cup	butter or margarine, softened	50 mL
1	package (250 g) cream cheese, softened	1
3 cups	milk	750 mL
1	package (153 g) vanilla instant pudding	1
1 cup	whipping cream, whipped* Gummy worms	250 mL

Whiz cookies in blender or food processor until they look like dirt.

In a medium bowl, cream butter and cream cheese.

In another bowl, combine milk and pudding mix. Beat about 2 minutes or until it begins to thicken. Add cream cheese mixture, beating until smooth. Fold in whipped cream.

Layer "dirt" and cream cheese mixture in an 8-cup (2 L) bowl, placing gummy worms strategically throughout. Finish with a layer of "dirt." Serve in "sandpails" with "shovels."

Makes 8 - 12 servings.

* 2 cups (500 mL) whipped topping may be substituted.

Cookie Birthday Party

Prepare a basic rolled cookie dough such as Paintbrush Cookies, Sour Cream Sugar Cookies, Gingerbread Cookies, Hanukkah Cookies or Holiday Cut-Out Cookies. Lightly flour the kitchen table, round up several cookie cutters, and set out candies, icing and other decorations. Let the kids go to it. Cool the baked cookies and put into bags to go home with their creators.

Cookie Friends

Fun for kids to make and give.

Refrigerator cookie dough, chilled (p 94)
Candies and icing for decorating (optional)

Preheat oven to 375°F (190°C).

Slice chilled dough. Follow diagrams below to cut cookies into required pieces, or create your own designs. Arrange pieces, barely touching, on ungreased cookie sheet as shown. Press in tiny candies for eyes, if desired.

Bake for 8 minutes or until lightly browned. Let cool on cookie sheet for about 3 minutes, then transfer to racks to cool. Decorate with icing, if desired.

Cone and Cookie Clowns

Guaranteed to please!

20 large round cookies*, crackers or wafers
1 carton (2 L) ice cream or sorbet
20 ice cream cones
Pieces of dried and candied fruit and small
things (cold cereals, chocolate chips, etc) to
make eyes, ears, mouth and nose

Place a large rounded scoop of ice cream in centre of each cookie, pressing lightly to secure. Place cone, wide end down, on top of ice cream to make a hat. Add garnishes to form eyes, ears, mouth and nose. Freeze until serving time.

Makes 20.

* Many of the recipes in this book would be suitable. Possibilities include Gingerbread Cookies, Snickerdoodles, Coconut Sugar Cookies, Holiday Cut-Out Cookies, or Sour Cream Sugar Cookies.

Variation:

Use small cookies and mini cones to make miniature clowns.

Cookies with a Purpose

Cooking-Making with Kids

Cooking with kids can be a most enjoyable and rewarding experience. Of course the natural motivation for everyone is eating the finished cookies, as well as samples of the dough along the way. Here are a few things to keep in mind when cooking with boys and girls:

- Choose a simple, basic recipe with inexpensive ingredients and flavours that children enjoy. Children are very disappointed if the cookies do not turn out, so it is suggested that the recipe be tested first. Children love to roll dough and use a variety of cookie cutters to make new shapes. Let them be creative.
- Allow plenty of time when there are few interruptions. Accept the mess and the sticky spoons. Aim for the fun of doing the recipe together. Don't worry if the cookies are not all perfect.
- Repeat the same recipe several times. Children feel more confident if they have successfully completed the recipe before. As children grow older they can do more of the job — from dumping ingredients at age two or three, to operating the electric mixer at age five, to making the complete recipe at age eleven. Young children may lose interest before the last cookie is baked, so be prepared to finish up alone.
- Encourage children to help with the cleanup and expect more of them as they grow older.
- Be sure to serve the cookies at the next family meal with lots of praise for the new cook.

Many of our recipes are suitable for making with kids. Here are some to get you started:

91	Choco Chunkies
40	Chocolate Crackles
56	Chocolate Valentine Hearts
28	Coconut Sugar Cookies
52	Gingerbread Cookies
30	Holiday Cut-Outs
121	The Monster Batch
107	Oat Munchers
184	Paintbrush Cookies
117	Peanut Butter Cookies
96	Snickerdoodles

Cookies with Messages

Baking cookies for someone, in itself, sends a subtle caring message. But sometimes, it's nice to make the message more obvious. Here are some ways to do this.

- Decorate cut-out cookies with a heart or happy face. This is a sure way to bring out the smiles.
- Write the person's name on a cookie. Its surprising how personalized cookies touch the hearts of both adults and children.
- Insert a written message into a cookie. Some commercial fortune cookies have enough of an opening for you to remove their message and replace it with yours. Or make the rolled version of our Lace Cookies and tuck in a message. Write out your own messages, or photocopy this page and use the ones below.
- Draw a heart in the filling before putting on the top cookie when making filled cookies. The person receiving the cookie won't see it, but you'll know it's there!

I love you.	You make my heart sing!
You belong in the world.	You are loved as you are.
You have a wonderful gift to share with the world.	You warm my heart!
Your needs are important to me.	You are needed in the world.
You light up my life!	I love who you are.
I love you even when we differ.	

Cookie Exchanges

A cookie exchange is an enjoyable, time-saving way of adding variety to your cookie supply. Each contributor bakes one large batch of a favourite cookie or bar, and comes away with smaller quantities of several friends' favourites. The exchange can be an evening social gathering or a morning coffee party. In any event, it can be a fruitful and fun opportunity for getting together with old friends. Usually an exchange is organized before Christmas to streamline holiday baking. However, an enthusiastic group could do the same thing any time of the year.

Organization
An effective exchange requires some advance planning. To ensure an equitable exchange, the group will need answers to these questions.
- *How many participants will there be?* This will determine how many cookies each person has to make and package.
- *Who will be making what?* This ensures variety, and that the needs of participants are met.
- *What constitutes a fair exchange?* Factors such as complicated preparation and expensive ingredients need to be accounted for. Sometimes a one-for-one exchange ratio is not appropriate.
- *How will the exchanging of cookies take place?* There are several possibilities — at a coffee party, in a central location one evening, or through a pick-up and delivery arrangement.
- *When will the exchange take place?* If everything can be frozen, it could occur comfortably ahead of the busy holiday season.

Packaging the Cookies
Cookies should be packaged in durable containers that need not be returned. Small boxes, plastic baskets and tubs, or styrofoam and foil pans from convenience foods can be saved throughout the year. If not airtight, they will need to be over-wrapped with plastic. Add a label, and a holiday ribbon if desired.

Storing the Cookies
Cookies should be prepared shortly before the exchange so the recipient will receive cookies at their best, with maximum storage life left. Label packages with any special storage instructions — e.g. use within 3 days, may be frozen for up to a month, needs a week before serving.

Cookies for Camping and Picnics

Cookies for outdoor events like camping and picnics need to carry well. Cookies that look beautiful on a tea or Christmas plate may be too fragile for carrying long distances. Soft drop cookies, oatmeal cookies, and bars and squares transport well. It is usually preferrable to leave them uniced.

Layer cookies and pre-cut bars in cookie tins or plastic containers, placing sheets of wax paper between the layers. Baking pans with lids make ideal travel containers for bars — simply carry uncut bars, covered, in the pan in which they were baked.

Some examples of cookies and bars that travel well:

97	Applesauce Oatmeal Cookies
98	Banana Drop Cookies
114	Butterscotch Oaties
103	Chewy Bars
100	Chewy Coconut Macaroons
124	Chocolate Chip Date Bars
91	Choco Chunkies
115	Cracker Jack Cookies
111	Dad's Cookies
41	Date Cherry Cookies
93	Easy Date-Filled Oatmeal Cookies
151	Food for the Gods
171	Fruit Bars
134	Fudge Brownies
102	Golden Gems
55	Halloween Hermits
108	Honey Raisin Cookies
121	Monster Batch
163	Peanut Butter Biggies
165	Power Cookies
123	Rolled Oat Drop Cookies
110	Sesame Seed Cookies

Cookies — Quick and Easy

Quick and easy recipes are *popular* with most of us and *needed* by many of us. With this in mind, we gave considerable thought to making every recipe in this book as quick and easy as possible. We did so by:
- developing a clear, consistent writing style.
- streamlining the methods. For example, whenever possible, the recipes use only one bowl. We add the baking powder or soda, salt and flavourings directly to the creamed mixture instead of combining it with the flour in a second bowl. This saves a bowl and a step. It has the added advantage of ensuring even distribution of these ingredients.

Bar Cookies
Bar cookies, we think, must have been the inspiration of a busy mom who decided to press the cookie dough into a pan and bake it all at once rather than taking the time to make individual cookies.

The quickest, easiest bars are those which:
- contain few ingredients
- use ingredients that do not require further cutting, chopping, melting, etc.
- are mixed in one bowl
- are one layer only
- are left uniced

Unbaked Cookies
These can be a close second, time-wise, as they require no attention once they have been dropped, shaped or spread in a pan. Check ingredient list and method, though, as some are fussy to make.

Baked Cookies
Baking individual cookies obviously takes more time than baking bars. Drop cookies are faster than shaped ones, and shaped are faster than rolled.

To make maximum use of your time, prepare cookie dough one day and bake the following day or later in the week. Keep dough well wrapped and refrigerated until ready to use. This can be done with drop cookies as well as those that are rolled and shaped.

Refrigerator cookies are the original "make now — bake later" cookie. The dough is shaped into rolls, wrapped well, and refrigerated or frozen until needed. It is then cut and baked — no dropping, shaping or rolling required.

Any cookie dough stiff enough to shape into a roll can become a "refrigerator cookie." Experiment a little!

Quick and Easy Recipes in this Book
We had planned to list quick and easy recipes, but the list was far too long. In addition, it became unbelievably complicated when we tried to divide it into fast, faster and fastest categories! It seemed that our plan to make "quick and easy" an inherent part of this book had worked. So, instead of a long list, we decided it would be most useful if we included the preceding information to help you determine which are quick and easy recipes.

Quick and easy recipes are found throughout this book. To help you find what you are looking for, the back of each colour photo has a listing according to type of cookies in that section. For example, if you are looking for bars, you'll find a listing of all the bars in this book by quickly scanning those pages.

Cookies for Giving

A gift of food can be a gift of love. We are not saying that food can ever replace love; in fact it is a serious mistake to use any food as a substitute for love. But food prepared and given *with* love warms the hearts of both the giver and receiver.

Decorated boxes, bright paper plates, colourful baskets and decorated sandwich bags make good carriers. Create your own "designer" containers by covering boxes and used plastic containers — including their lids — with self-adhesive paper. Paper serviettes and doilies can serve as colourful liners. Keep the trappings simple — it's the food itself that counts.

We think all the recipes in the book are good enough to give. However, here are some specific suggestions:

Cookies for Mailing

Receiving a gift of cookies in the mail provides immense joy to the recipient, all the more so if they arrive intact. A box full of crumbs is a disappointing sight, so choose cookies that travel well. Soft cookies, drop cookies and bars generally keep well and travel best. Avoid fragile or brittle cookies. Eliminate frosted and sandwich-type filled cookies; they are sticky and difficult to pack.

There are several choices for containers. Ready-made cookie tins and plastic storage containers are attractive. Used plastic containers or a sturdy cardboard box may also serve the purpose — as-is or covered with attractive self-adhesive paper.

Line the container with moisture-proof wrapping, and pad the bottom with crumpled wax paper or paper towels, or shredded newspaper. Wrap cookies individually (or two back-to-back) in moisture-proof wrapping and pack in layers. Put more crumpled or shredded paper between the packages, and a final layer on top. If using a tin or plastic container, place it in a sturdy cardboard box, padding it with paper so it can't move.

Bars can be baked in a foil pan and left in the pan for mailing. Cover with foil taped to the pan. Place in a sturdy mailing box, cushioning the pan on all sides with crumpled paper towels or newspaper.

Some examples of cookies to mail include:

19	Almond Shortcake
173	Apricot Almond Bars
120	Big and Chewy Chocolate Chippers
103	Chewy Bars
168	Chewy Ginger Cookies
143	Fig Bars
27	Lebkuchen
165	Power Cookies
172	Seed Bars
174	Wonder Bars

Index

by recipe name

by special dietary characteristics

Recipes without dairy products

Recipes without eggs

This book is meant to be given

... to a **favourite person** on Valentine's day, with a batch of Chocolate Valentine Hearts or San Francisco Fudge Foggies — accompanied by lots of love.

... as a **shower gift**, along with a cookie sheet. Personalize the book by writing in your favourite cookie recipes and household hints.

... to **parents of young children**, not only for the recipes, but also for the many ideas and ways to involve kids in cookie-making.

... to a **young person** who has moved away from home; the recipes are easy to follow, even for inexperienced cooks. Write your family favourites in some of the blank spaces.

... to **grandparents** of preschool children; there are many wonderful ideas for do-together projects that encourage creativity.

... to your child's **teacher**. Your child can help bake a batch of cookies to go with it — a marvellous way for children to feel they're part of the giving process.

... as a **hostess gift**; it's a delightful way of saying thank you.

... at **Christmas, Thanksgiving, Halloween, Easter, Mother's Day...or anytime.** Bake a batch of cookies, put them in a cookie jar or tin, and include a copy of this book.

Your favourites

Children's Cottage Cookie Cook Book

...more favourites